SUPER INTERESTING
IRELAND
FACTS AND ACTIVITIES

Super Interesting Ireland Facts & Activities

355 Fun Facts, Engaging Worksheets, Puzzles, Word Searches, Coloring, & Drawing for Smart Kids

Henry Bennett

Liberstax Publishing, London, United Kingdom.

🐏 **Liberstax Publishing**

To leave an Amazon review please visit https://www.amazon.com/ryp or scan the QR code below...

Table of Contents

Introduction

Welcome! Or should I say, *fáilte*!

My name is Henry Bennett, and it's my great pleasure to welcome you to another facts book.

I hope you're ready to learn because this time, we're learning more than 300 super interesting facts about Ireland, and we have lots of beautiful and historic ground to cover!

We're going to learn facts about everything Ireland-related, including

- its lush landscapes and natural beauty!

- some myths and folklore, including the mythical world of banshees, fairies, and leprechauns!

- the Giant's Causeway, a beautiful natural wonder found in Northern Ireland!

- tales of Vikings and castles!

- the stories behind St. Patrick's Day, as well as other Irish holidays!

- classic Irish music and dancing!

- traditional Gaelic games!

- the Gaelic language!

- famous Irish eats!

- Ireland's ancient treasure!

- Irish inventions!

- potatoes of all shapes and sizes!

- the resilience of Northern Ireland!

- Ireland's zoos and wildlife parks!

- the meanings and history of Celtic art and symbols!

- Irish folklore and a bedtime story or two!

- famous Irish landmarks!

- traditional Irish crafts!

- the Burren, an incredible limestone landscape!

- Irish schools and education!

- Irish pop culture, including movies and TV shows!

- Irish seas!

- Ireland's ancient ruins!

- Irish lighthouses!

And much, much more!

I can't promise that you will be fluent in Gaelic or a master of Irish dancing by the end of this book, but I can promise that you will know a *lot* about Ireland!

So, throw on your favorite green jumper and grab a green pen and a pad (okay, that might be a little too much) or maybe it isn't? Because Ireland is jam-packed with wonders to discover!

Let's go, kids—Chapter 1 will give you all an introduction to Ireland!

Chapter 1: An Introduction to Ireland!

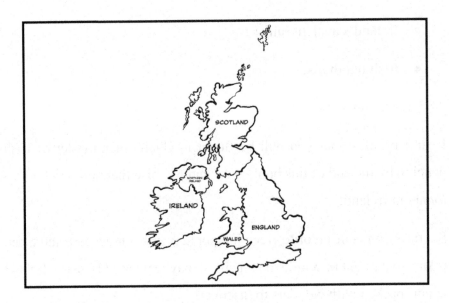

Let's kick things off with 10 quick-fire facts to introduce us to Ireland!

1. Ireland is an island nation that is found in the West of Europe! Eighty percent of Ireland is made up of the Republic of Ireland, and the other 20% of the land that's found in the North is called Northern Ireland! The whole island is divided into a total of 32 separate counties!

2. Ireland is the second biggest island in the British Isles and the third biggest island in Europe!

3. Ireland was nicknamed the "Emerald Isle" because of its wide and lush green open fields!

4. Ireland is also covered in lots of mountains and rocky land, which was left behind after the thick glaciers it was covered in melted more than 15,000 years ago!

5. Today, more than 5 million people call Ireland home!

6. Ireland loves animals so much that their earliest coins used to have their pictures on them!

7. It's believed that Ireland was founded between 6000 and 3500 B.C.E. The Celts arrived from Europe around 700 B.C.E. and lived on the island for almost 2,000 years before the Vikings arrived!

8. Ireland has a rich history of agriculture and farming!

9. The Irish flag consists of three thick horizontal stripes that are green, white, and orange!

10. Ireland has two major mountain ranges, and five major rivers—and we will learn more about them all later!

(*Ireland Facts: All About the Emerald Isle*, n.d.)

I think that's you all suitably introduced to the Emerald Isle, so let's move on!

Chapter 2 is all about Irish myths and folklore!

Chapter 2: A Land of Legends

Next, we'll look at some Irish myths and folklore, including banshees, fairies, and leprechauns!

1. The banshee is an Irish mythological creature that looks like an old lady. Her piercing scream is supposed to mean something bad is supposed to happen, like the death of a family member—chilling!

2. The story of the *Salmon of Knowledge* tells the tale of a magical fish that contains all of the knowledge of the world and the promise of that knowledge being given to whoever eats it!

3. *The Cattle Raid of Cooley* is a story about a Celtic goddess called Queen Medb who argued that she had more money than

her husband, but when she realized he had a champion bull, she started a battle with a cattle owner to get one of her own!

4. King Lir was the ruler of the Irish Sea who had four children with his wife, Eva. When Eva passed, Lir married her sister, Aoife, who became jealous of the time that the children spent with their dad and cursed them to spend the next 900 years as swans!

5. Changelings are naughty fairies that replace human babies! They can look unhealthy or disfigured, so sometimes parents worry that their children look unwell because they've actually been replaced by them! Changelings are believed to have special powers!

6. Morrigan was also a shapeshifter, but rather than being a mischievous little deviant, she was a powerful Celtic goddess who ruled over ancient Ireland!

7. *The Pursuit of Diarmuid and Grainne* is a love story about two people who fell in love at first sight. The only problem is that they met at Grainne's wedding! After spiking the drinks of everyone in attendance, the lovers went on the run but were chased down by a group of Irish folklore's most mighty warriors, the Fianna, led by the man Grainne was supposed to marry. In most stories, peace was finally made between Diarmuid and the Fianna—love wins!

8. Have you ever heard of the Abhartach? What about if I tell you that this ancient creature is also known as the Irish vampire?

Irish legend tells of this blood-sucking ancestor of Dracula. He was believed to be a dwarf and possess magical powers!

9. Leprechauns are small faerie folk similar to elves. They are believed to wear emerald green and hide valuable pots of gold that they must hand over if they are caught—but nobody can catch them!

10. The pooka is a mischievous fairy that can shapeshift and often changes into a black horse with fiery eyes! While the pooka is known for playing pranks on humans, it's also believed to protect animals and help lost travelers find their way!

(O'Hara, 2024; *Leprechauns*, n.d.; *Irish Fairies: Irish Folklore, Myth & Legend*, 2023)

Ireland is a country with a truly magical history and the facts above have only scratched the surface!

Next up are some facts on one of Ireland's most incredible natural phenomena, the Giant's Causeway!

Chapter 3: The Giant's Causeway

Let's dive into 10 facts about one of Northern Ireland's geological wonders!

1. The Giant's Causeway was created by volcanic eruptions. Once the lava left behind cooled down, it left the amazing hexagonal-shaped pillars behind, meaning that the Causeway is made of volcanic rock more than 60 million years old!

2. The mythological and much cooler explanation for the Causeway is that an Irish giant tore pieces of the coast to create a bridge to Scotland so that it could challenge a Scottish giant to a duel. The Causeway is said to be what was left of the bridge!

3. The Causeway was first discovered in the 17th century by the Bishop of Derry, and it was so unique that no one could decide if it had been created by humans or nature!

4. Some of the Causeway can still be found in Scotland, too; Fingal's Cave is 278 feet long and lined with basalt columns of its own!

5. The Causeway is made up of around 40,000 individual columns, but they aren't all hexagonal, some have up to eight points!

6. The strange landscape of the Causeway has created a habitat that has attracted lots of different birds, such as fulmars, eiders, redshanks, and cormorants!

7. The volcano that created that Causeway has now eroded away and vanished from the face of the Earth. So, who's to say that it wasn't the Giants instead? Just kidding!

8. The Causeway offers a hiking trail that is made of 162 stone steps and leads to an amazing view of the basalt columns from above. There's also a hiking trail called Causeway Coast Way that takes hikers along the stunning coast!

9. The type of rock that the columns are made from is called "tholeiitic basalt" and it's also found on the moon!

10. The Causeway has been given lots of nicknames, such as "the organ pipes," "the camel's humps," the "honeycomb," "the

eyes of the giants," "the harp," and "the chimneys." Whatever people choose to call it, it's beautiful!

(*The Giants Causeway in 10 Amazing Facts*, 2021; *10 Surprising Facts About the Giant's Causeway You Probably Didn't Know!*, 2023)

Who else wants to visit the Giant's Causeway? I know I do!

Let's move on to our next chapter—a place that I have been lucky enough to visit—the Irish capital of Dublin!

Chapter 4: Dublin's Rich History and Exciting Future

Chapter 4 will explore 10 facts that are all about Dublin!

1. Dublin is the capital city of the Republic of Ireland and is located on the country's east coast.

2. Dublin was founded way back in 841 by Vikings and quickly became one of the most important and well-known Viking settlements!

3. Dublin's Viking history runs so deep that it is home to the biggest Viking cemetery outside of Scandinavia (where the Vikings came from), which is made up of 40 Viking graves!

4. The name "Dublin" comes from the old Irish Celtic term "Dubh Linn," which meant "Black Pool" and was inspired by a deep, filthy pool in Dublin Castle—gross!

5. Dublin is home to Ireland's oldest library, Marsh's Library, which was opened in 1707. Today, the library is home to more than 25,000 books that date back as far as the 16th century for more than 23,000 yearly visitors to enjoy!

6. When the Rotunda Hospital was built in Dublin in 1745, it became the first hospital built in Europe that had one purpose—delivering babies!

7. Dublin is home to the widest street in Europe; it's called O'Connell Street and measures a crazy 160 feet in length!

8. We can't talk about O'Connell Street without mentioning O'Connell Bridge, which is one of Dublin's most popular landmarks. It's popular because of the bizarre fact that it's wider than it is long and it's the only bridge in Europe that has this weird feature!

9. Today, Dublin is the technology hub of Europe. Tech giants like Etsy, Facebook, and Google, all have their European headquarters there!

10. *The Guinness Book of Records* was created in Dublin by the managing director of a Guinness brewery. What started as a bit of a marketing giveaway soon became a worldwide phenomenon!

(Whitnear, n.d.; Ó Murchadh, 2023; Pauline, 2023)

Dublin is a place full of wonder, fun, and history!

Speaking of history, our next chapter is about another one of Ireland's historical landmarks, the Cliffs of Moher, so let's go!

Chapter 5: The Cliffs of Moher

Let's explore some facts about the historic Cliffs of Moher, shall we?

1. The Cliffs are visited by more than 1 million tourists every single year making them one of Ireland's most popular attractions!

2. Those tourists have a lot to look at, too; the Cliffs rise as high as 702 feet tall and are 8.6 miles long!

3. The formation of the Cliffs of Moher started more than 300 million years ago when heavy rainfall caused flooding that poured mud and sand into rivers that carried it into the sea. Over millions of years, that mud and sand solidified to become the formation that we see today!

4. The Cliffs of Moher are home to a rock formation that is called "Hag's Head." "Hag" is a word for an old woman and the formation looks like a woman looking out to sea! The story goes that a woman chased the man she loved out across the Cliffs but she fell into the sea below!

5. The Cliffs are *full* of nature! Over 30,000 sea birds are known to breed there, including some endangered species!

6. There are so many seabirds, in fact, that the Cliffs host a seabird festival every single year for those who want to get up close and take pictures—puffins are proving to be a big hit!

7. That's not all—the Cliffs are home to lots of hares and goats, *and* dolphins, whales, and seals can all be spotted in the water below!

8. The Cliffs have been attracting tourists since the 16th century when travel writers would come to visit!

9. O'Brien's Tower is a tower that was built on the cliff edge in the 19th century by a landowner named Cornelius O'Brien, who saw the opportunity to make some cash from the beautiful views!

10. The bottom of the Cliffs is made of the oldest rock and the multicolored layers of rock get younger the further you move up the Cliff!

(Janet, 2016; *The Cliffs of Moher*, n.d.)

That wraps up our look at the majestic Cliffs of Moher!

Our next chapter will be just as majestic as we take a look at the history of Irish castles and the royalty who lived in them!

Chapter 6: Irish Castles—Stories of Ancient Kings and Queens

THE BLARNEY STONE

Let's dive into some tales of Irish castles and the kings and queens that lived within them!

1. Today, Ireland is home to more than 30,000 castles, including castle ruins, and they date as far back as the 12th century!

2. The original foundations of Blarney Castle date all the way back to 1210! Those foundations were destroyed in 1446, before being rebuilt by Cormac Laidir MacCarthy into the version that still stands today!

3. The Blarney Stone is a block of limestone that is found in the castle, and it's believed to have magical powers that were given

to it by a witch who cast a spell on it to thank a king who saved her from drowning!

4. Today, visitors from all around the world visit Blarney Castle so they can kiss the Blarney Stone and hopefully enjoy the powers of the "gift of the gab," which basically means you can talk a lot and persuade people!

5. Kilkenny Castle was built in 1260 by the first Earl of Pembroke and was the home of the Butler family until the middle of the 20th century!

6. The Butler family is known for bravely withstanding a siege during the Irish Civil War in their bedroom with a machine gun outside of their bedroom door!

7. The oldest castle in Ireland is the Trim Castle in County Meath. It was built in the 12th century as a keep for Hugh de Lacy, who was the first Lord of Meath and the fourth Baron of Lacy!

8. Dunluce Castle is found near the Giant's Causeway and was originally built in the 13th century. It is believed to have inspired C.S Lewis to write the *Chronicles of Narnia*!

9. The Rock of Cashel is a castle that was built back in the 12th century. Legend has it that the castle was created when the devil took a bite of a mountain called "Devil's Bit" and a piece fell out of his mouth!

10. Donegal Castle was built back in 1213 and was owned by one of the most powerful Gaelic Irish families between the 5th and 16th centuries—the O'Donnells!

(*Fun Facts about Blarney Castle*, 2011; *Kilkenny Castle: 10 Amazing Facts About an Ancient Irish Structure*, n.d.; Derry, 2023)

Amazing! The stories of these castles, and their regal roots, opens the doors to a time that we could only imagine before, isn't history amazing?

Chapter 7 will take a turn towards another incredible moment in history, the construction of the Titanic, which you might be surprised to know took place on Irish soil!

Chapter 7: The Titanic

Let's learn some facts about the iconic Titanic's famous roots and Belfast's shipbuilding history!

1. The Titanic was designed in 1907 by Thomas Andrews, an Irishman from Northern Irish County, County Down!

2. Construction of the ship took place at the Harland and Wolff shipyard in Belfast and started in 1907, taking three years to complete!

3. The ship took around 3,000 workers to complete and cost $7.5 million, which is around $200 million in today's money!

4. Building the ship was such a big project that it created over 3,000 new jobs in the city of Belfast and boosted their economy—talk about a huge bonus!

5. Once finished, the ship was a whopping 882 feet and 6 inches long and weighed a scale-busting 46,000 tons!

6. Cobh, in County Cork, was the final pick-up for the ship's passengers, and the ship was so big that passengers from Cobh had to board using smaller ships that took them aboard!

7. Of the 123 passengers that boarded the Titanic from Cobh, 113 of them were third class, seven were second class, and just three traveled first class!

8. If you visit Belfast today, you'll be able to visit an award-winning attraction that lets visitors walk through the design, construction, and operation of the ship!

9. An interactive experience in Cobh allows visitors to walk in the footsteps of the passengers who boarded there!

10. Sadly, 110 Irish people lost their lives on the Titanic, including Edward Pomeroy Colley, who passed away on his 37th birthday. Fifty-four Irish people did survive the tragic accident though, including Francis Brown, who luckily departed in Cobh!

(*Titanic's Irish Roots*, 2019; *Cobh: Titanic's Last Port of Call*, 2022; Kennedy, 2023)

The story of the Titanic, although it is ultimately a sad one, is also an incredible example of Ireland's fantastic engineering industry and the ship's construction is something they are rightfully proud of.

Our next chapter is about something else that I'm sure they're proud of, but for very different reasons—St. Patrick's Day!

Chapter 8: St. Patrick's Day

Let's learn all about the fun of St. Patrick's Day!

1. St. Patrick's Day is a yearly celebration of St. Patrick, a former slave who rose to become the first bishop of Ireland!

2. Although St. Patrick's Day is an Irish holiday, it's now celebrated all around the world. It includes lots of eating, drinking, dancing, and of course, the color green!

3. In Chicago, the Chicago River has been dyed green to celebrate the holiday every year since 1962! Sometimes, even the White House dyes its fountain water green in celebration!

4. Legend has it that St. Patrick drove all of the snakes out of Ireland, which may sound like an exaggeration, but that's the beautiful thing about legends!

5. A shamrock, or clover, is a three-leaf clover that represents both Ireland and St. Patrick's Day. The clover represents love, hope, and faith! Finding a four-leaf one is supposed to be extremely lucky!

6. One of the most fun traditions of St. Patrick's Day is the belief that if you don't wear green on the day, you'll be pinched by a cheeky little leprechaun! There'll be lots of them around, too, because leprechauns are the most popular thing for celebrators to dress up as!

7. It's traditional to eat Irish foods like cabbage, corned beef, shepherd's pie, and Irish soda bread on St. Patrick's Day.

8. As crazy as it sounds now, St. Patrick's Day wasn't always about the color green! Up until 1798, it was the color blue that was associated with St. Patrick! The color green was first used as an opportunity to rebel!

9. The Guinness Book of World Records calls St. Patrick's Day the friendliest of the year! How lovely is that?

10. St. Patrick's Day has lots of different nicknames, including "St. Patty's Day," "the Feast of Saint Patrick," and "St. Paddy's Day."

(Top 10 Facts About Saint Patrick's Day!, n.d; Griffin, 2021)

St. Patrick's Day is a wonderful, worldwide event that brings happy people together!

Our next chapter will look at something else that brings people together—traditional Irish music and dancing, a lot of which will be taking place during St. Patrick's Day festivals!

Chapter 9: Traditional Irish Music and Dance

Let's dive into some facts about traditional Irish music and dancing!

1. The Irish love music so much that the Celtic harp (which has been played since the 10th century) is on their Euro coins today!

2. Irish step dance is a form of dance that involves keeping your upper body as stiff as a board while performing crazy footwork sequences. Step dancers either wear hard tap-dancing shoes or soft ballet shoes, depending on the type of performance!

3. The uilleann pipes are the Irish version of bagpipes but the two of them are very different! Where the Scottish bagpipes are inflated by a player breathing into them, uilleann pipes are pumped to inflation using a device instead, before they're

squeezed to produce the music. Uilleann pipe players can sing while they play!

4. The bodhran is a traditional Irish frame drum that is played with a small stick called a "beater" or with the player's hand!

5. While Americans learn to play the recorder at school, Irish schoolchildren are taught to play the tin whistle!

6. Lilting is a traditional form of Gaelic singing that sounds and looks like traditional jazz scat music. It involves a lot of lyrics that make little sense and words that don't sound like words. The Irish love it, though, and you will, too, once you've searched it up on YouTube!

7. The roots of Irish dancing go all the way back to over 2,000 years ago when an ancient tribe called the Celts used to use dance to tell stories, perform rituals, and enjoy celebrations!

8. Riverdance is very popular now, but it wasn't actually introduced to the rest of the world until 1994 when it was featured at the Eurovision Song Contest. Today, there are Irish dance schools and competitions in countries around the globe!

9. Irish dancing competitions have been a part of Irish culture for many years with the first one taking place in the Irish capital of Dublin in 1897!

10. Irish music existed before 1700 and was influenced by Irish history. Today, it's become a blend of pop, modern rock, and a little bit of country and bluegrass!

(*17 Fascinating Facts About Irish Music*, 2013; *7 Facts About Irish Dance*, n.d.)

Who's up for a dance, then?

If dancing isn't your thing, sports might be, and Chapter 10 is all about traditional Gaelic games!

Chapter 10: Gaelic Games—Hurling and Gaelic Football

It's time to learn 10 facts about hurling and Gaelic football, two of Ireland's favorite sports!

1. Gaelic football first appeared in Irish records back in 1308!

2. The Gaelic Athletics Association, or GAA, was founded in 1884 to support the growth of the sport, and today it has more than 1 million members!

3. Today, Gaelic football is the most popular sport across Ireland, and its national final packs stadiums with 80,000 fans every year!

4. Gaelic football is a mixture of rugby, basketball, and soccer, but unlike the latter, it has no offside rule!

5. Even the Gaelic football players at the highest level aren't actually paid for playing and play for the love of the game! I know a few sports that could learn from their attitude and commitment!

6. With a crazy 38 championship titles, Kerry is the most successful Gaelic football team of all time!

7. Hurling first appeared in the Olympics back in 1904. The gold medal was won by the Innisfail Hurling Club!

8. Hurling is incredibly popular, too, with 82,000 fans attending the All-Ireland Hurling Final every year!

9. Hurling is known as the fastest field sport, with the ball being hit at speeds of over 100 miles per hour. Thankfully, the players are required to wear helmets and safety pads!

10. The "hurl" is the stick the game is played with. It looks similar to an ice hockey stick, but the two are used much differently, with a ball being balanced on the hurling stick instead of being pushed along the ground!

11. Speaking of ice hockey, the word "puck" actually came from the Irish word "poc," which is the word used for striking a ball with a hurl!

12. Some believe that hurling was invented to train warriors in the Middle Ages, which may well be true because the Marine Corps has two teams of their own and they are indeed modern-day warriors!

(Hofer, 2023; *11 Fun Facts about Hurling*, 2015)

Who's feeling competitive now? Ireland has a storied sporting history, and the Irish are very proud of their sports, as they should be!

Our next chapter is an introduction to the Irish language of Gaelic!

Chapter 11: The Irish Language—An Introduction to Gaelic

Let's dive into the traditional Irish language of Gaelic, from its historic origins to a fun phrase or two!

1. The Gaelic language doesn't include words for "yes" or "no!" Instead, when they're asked a question that needs a yes or no answer, they do a little explaining instead. For example, if they were offered a drink, they would say "I don't want a drink," instead of just "no."

2. Their language is a little different than most. When they explain something, they have seen or done, they start with a verb (doing word). For example, we might say "I saw a bird," but they would say, "Saw I a bird."

3. There are different words for numbers depending on whether they are counting humans, animals, or doing math!

4. Most people in Ireland spoke Irish until Ireland joined the United Kingdom in 1801! At this point, state schools that had only taught Irish had to start teaching children the English language!

5. Only around one percent of the whole country actually speaks Gaelic!

6. Let's count to 10 in Gaelic!

   o aon (a-n)

   o do (doe)

   o tri (tree)

   o ceathair (cah-her)

   o cuig (coo-igg)

   o se (shay)

   o seacht (shocked)

   o ocht (uk-ed)

   o naoi (knee)

   o deich (de)

7. A small Irish community that mostly speaks Gaelic is called a "Gaeltacht," and they tend to have their own version of some

words, too. They're like little towns that speak their own secret languages, and schoolchildren are taken on trips to them to work on their Gaelic!

8. Irish Gaelic is what's called an Indo-European language, meaning it evolved from some of the earliest forms of human language, making it one of the oldest languages across Europe!

9. Despite its rich history, today, Gaelic is an endangered language, meaning it's at risk of dying out!

10. Irish Gaelic isn't just spoken in Ireland, it's also spoken across other parts of the United Kingdom, including Scotland!

(*8 Fun Facts about the Irish Language*, 2015; *Irish Language Facts for Kids*, n.d.; Wickham, 2020b)

Isn't learning new languages fun? It can also be a little tricky!

Our next chapter will leave worrying about languages to some of the most influential Irish writers and poets!

Chapter 12: Irish Writers and Poets

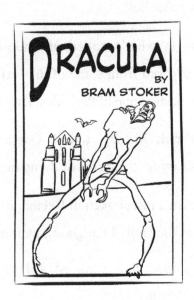

We're going to look at some of Ireland's most influential writers and poets next, as well as some of their work!

1. Oscar Wilde was born in Dublin in 1854. He is one of the most famous and influential writers and poets to have ever grabbed a pen. One of his famous works includes, *The Importance of Being Earnest.*

2. Maeve Binchy was born in Dublin in 1940. She wrote novels and plays that were all about celebrating Irish life, and they were so popular that they sold more than 40 million copies around the world!

3. Bram Stoker was also born in Dublin, but he was born in 1847. You know all about Stoker's work even if you've never heard

his name because he invented the blood-sucking fiend Count Dracula!

4. Edna O'Brien was born in Tuamgraney in 1930. She was an early supporter of equal rights for girls and was well ahead of her time in doing so. Her work gained her worldwide acclaim!

5. Jonathan Swift was born in Dublin way back in 1667. He is one of the English language's most influential writers, and his work has been adapted to modern times, including *Gulliver's Travels,* which starred Jack Black back in 2010!

6. W. B. Yeats was born in Dublin in 1865. He was a leading poet during the Irish literary revival of the late 19th century and is seen today as one of the most influential writers across all of 20th-century literature!

7. Eoin Colfer was born in Wexford. He is a world-famous children's author, meaning that many of you will have read some of his work! His most famous is the *Artemis Fowl* series!

8. C. S. Lewis was born in Belfast, in 1898. He created the classic Chronicles of Narnia series, which has been translated into 41 languages, sold more than 100 million copies, and has been adapted into television, movies, and just about any kind of media you could imagine!

9. James Joyce was born in Dublin in 1882. He is celebrated as one of the most influential writers of the early twentieth

century and his most famous work is a book called *Ulysses,* which he spent seven years writing!

(O'Hara, 2023; Wickham, 2020a)

The work of those featured in this chapter will stand the test of time, as will the recipes that are featured in the next. Chapter 13 is all about traditional Irish cuisine!

Chapter 13: Irish Cuisine

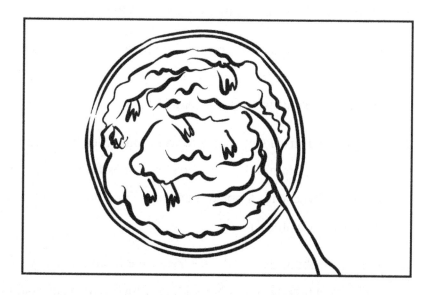

My stomach is growling already! Let's tuck into some facts about traditional Irish cuisine!

1. Soda bread is so popular in Ireland that most families have their own recipe for it! It's made with buttermilk, bicarbonate of soda, and flour and always has a deep cross cut into the top of it before baking to protect those eating it from evil spirits—delicious *and* spooky!

2. The Irish *love* potatoes, and it's a key ingredient in a lot of their traditional dishes, including colcannon, which is potatoes that are mashed with cabbage or kale!

3. Colcannon is also a Halloween tradition, and one of the most popular children's games at that time of year involves hiding a prize within it, with the winner believed to receive good luck!

4. A traditional Irish breakfast is huge and includes bacon, sausages, black and white pudding, grilled tomatoes, potato cakes, and eggs. How's that for a start to the day?!

5. Ireland's long coastline provides them with lots of seafood, so it's not surprising that seafood is a big part of their diet, from salmon and shellfish to salty seaweed!

6. A traditional Irish stew is made from mutton or lamb, carrots, onions, and potatoes. It's cooked slowly to soften the meat, and usually served with a potato pancake called boxty (I told you they loved potatoes!).

7. Let's talk about desserts! The Irish love to end a hearty meal with sweet bread and butter pudding, which is made by soaking bread in custard and then baking it until it turns crispy!

8. Another classic dessert is Irish whiskey cake, which is packed full of dried fruit and soaked in whiskey. Unfortunately, you'll have to wait until you're older to try it!

9. We all know that the Brits love a cup of tea, and the Irish are no different! It's polite to offer a mug of tea to any visitors, and it's preferred to be very strong (by leaving the tea bag in for a long time) before it's finished with a splash of milk!

10. Irish butter is made from grass-fed cow's milk and is known for being extra creamy and rich. They love spreading it over everything from sweet cakes to warm bread!

(*20 Surprising Facts About Irish Food You Probably Didn't Know*, 2023)

I'm starving! Let's all go and grab a snack before we move on to Chapter 14, shall we? It's all about the Book of Kells!

Chapter 14: The Book of Kells

It's time to unearth 10 facts about the Book of Kells, one of Ireland's most ancient pieces of treasure!

1. The Book of Kells is one of the most mysterious and magical treasures of Ireland. It's displayed in the library of Dublin's Trinity College and is visited by more than a million visitors every year!

2. No one actually knows where it was made! Some believe it was created in Kells, a small Irish town, while others think that it was started in Scotland and finished in Kells—mysterious!

3. One thing that we *do* know for sure, is that it was written by Colombian monks around the year 800!

4. The book is extremely valuable and was made from only the finest materials of the time, including 340 fine calfskin pages

and a combination of expensive pigments and gold for illustration!

5. The book was named after the Abbey of Kells, the monastery where it spent centuries!

6. When Oliver Cromwell led his army into Kells in 1654, the town's governor sent the Book of Kells to Dublin for safekeeping, and it's been there ever since!

7. The book was created for display and ceremonial purposes rather than to be read out loud. We know this because some of the writing within it is missing and other bits have been copied to fill it out—crafty!

8. So, what *is* in the Book of Kells? The four Gospels of the New Testament (Matthew, Mark, Luke, and John), summaries and passages, receipts for buildings, and a poem about a cat!

9. The public can't read the book and only a few of the beautiful pages are ever put on display at a time!

10. The book was created in a style called "Hiberno-Saxon style," which includes lots of bright colors, complicated patterns, and Irish-Celtic artwork and symbols!

(Roller, 2022; Harlitz-Kern, 2015)

The Book of Kells is truly magical!

Do you know what else is magical? Irish wildlife, which is what we're learning all about next!

Chapter 15: Irish Wildlife

Let's learn some facts about some of the wonderful wildlife that can be found in Ireland!

1. The wood mouse and the house mouse are the only two wild mouse species in the country!

2. There are only three amphibian species in Ireland: the natterjack toad, the common frog, and the smooth newt!

3. Red foxes are the largest species of fox and can mostly be found in Irish woodland. It's the only wild member of the dog family that's an Irish native!

4. The red squirrels found in Ireland are smaller and rarer than their gray companions!

5. The Irish coast is home to lots of marine animals, such as porpoises and seals. The coast is a busy breeding ground for seals, too, with thousands of pups born there every single year—cute!

6. The Irish hare is one of the oldest species in all of Ireland and can be quite hard to spot (despite being much bigger than rabbits). When it *is* spotted, it's usually grazing in the woods!

7. Irish setters are a breed of dog known for their beautiful red coat, although their coat actually used to be red and white!

8. Connemara ponies are beautiful in looks and in nature! These kind-hearted ponies are known for forming strong bonds with humans and for being incredibly gentle, too, despite being the largest breed of pony—making them gentle giants!

9. Minute pygmy shrews are the smallest mammal native to Ireland, measuring between a tiny 4.5 and 4.6 centimeters! They're so small, in fact, that people usually think they're mice when they spot them in long grass!

10. Great Irish elks were some of the largest deer to have lived in Ireland, once majestic, and towering, at over 6.5 feet in height. This is one mammal that is sadly now extinct (that means there are none left). Still, the legend of these elks lives on in Ireland, and their antlers and skeletons can be seen in museums!

11. Whether you believe Saint Patrick scared the snakes away from Ireland or not, the closest thing to a snake that the country has

to offer is the viviparous lizard! This lizard is the only one native to Ireland and is small with a long tail that it can regrow if it needs to!

12. Ireland's biggest land mammal, the red deer, is believed to have lived in Ireland for over 12,000 years and is its only native deer! They love the snow and are often spotted during the winter months!

(*10 Amazing Animal Species Native to Ireland*, 2024)

Isn't wildlife amazing? Ireland is a country that is blessed with some beautiful and unique species!

Our next chapter is all about some of the most creative and groundbreaking Irish inventions!

Chapter 16: Famous Irish Inventions

Let's learn about some of Ireland's most famous and coolest inventors and their inventions!

1. John Jolly was born near the village of Bracknagh and graduated from Dublin's Trinity College before inventing color photography in 1984—can you imagine all of your favorite pictures without color?

2. Louis Brennan, a man born in the town of Castlebar, invented the guided torpedo in 1877. His invention was so good that he was awarded funding by the British Navy!

3. A doctor from Dublin named Francis Rynd invented the hypodermic syringe (the syringes used to take blood tests) in 1844. Doctors still use his invention every single day!

4. The ejector seat was invented by Sir James Martin in 1946. The Royal Air Force (RAF) fitted all of their planes with them, and the invention is believed to have saved over 5,000 lives!

5. Submarines were invented by Irish school teacher John Philip Holland in 1878, and his invention won not one, not two, but three competitions held by the U.S. Navy!

6. A butcher from the Irish county of Waterford invented the bacon rasher in 1820. Before the rasher existed, bacon was eaten in large chunks—imagine how lumpy your bacon sandwiches would be!

7. The county of Waterford must have loved its food because the Jacobs family, who invented the cream cracker back in 1885, came from there, too! Cream crackers are now so popular that they're sold in over 35 countries around the world!

8. Joseph Murphy hated plain crisps so much that in 1954 he invented the cheese-and-onion-flavored crisp! His invention was such a hit that he became a millionaire, and now we have a *lot* of choices when it comes to crisps!

9. Irishman Hans Sloane invented chocolate milk back in the 17th century after he was inspired by the chocolate water that was being enjoyed in Jamaica. He first sold his tasty recipe as a medication!

10. In 1926, an Irish mechanic named Harry Ferguson invented the modern tractor. His design is still used on farms around the world today!

(*10 Irish Inventions That Changed the World*, 2015; *17 Weird and Wonderful Irish Inventions*, 2017).

How cool are some of those inventions?! Can you imagine life without chocolate milk?

Next, we'll take a look at some facts about a crucial part of Ireland's history—the potato famine!

Chapter 17: The Potato Famine

Let's look at some facts about the potato famine that helped shape Ireland's history!

1. Potatoes used to be the most important ingredient in Ireland, with most families having their own little potato farms that they used to feed themselves!

2. The potato famine was caused by a disease called blight, which infected and killed potatoes. It actually started in America in 1844 and had spread to Ireland within two years, infecting three-quarters of their crops!

3. The famine lasted four years in Ireland between 1845 and 1849!

4. Without potatoes to feed themselves, a lot of the Irish locals were forced to take dangerous journeys to other countries, and most of them chose America and Canada as their new homes!

5. As it often does, the world came together to help those struggling. Donations from all around the world were sent to Ireland to help them get through the famine, and the United States sent ships filled with clothes and food, too—sharing is caring!

6. Former British Prime Minister Sir Robert Peel tried to help the hungry Irish by providing corn kernels but didn't realize that they didn't have enough corn mills to handle it—whoops!

7. Unfortunately, many were left homeless by the famine, and many villages and towns were left completely empty!

8. The darkest year of the famine was called "Black 47." It took place in 1847 and sadly saw many who had been starving and homeless lose their lives!

9. One of Ireland's biggest mistakes during the famine was the decision to continue to send food grown on their land to other countries. This process is called exporting and while it may have made the country money, it saw precious food leave when the locals needed it the most!

10. In total, it's believed that the famine took the lives of more than 1 million Irish people, making the country's recovery and modern-day success a truly amazing comeback story!

(Roller, 2021; Hesse, 2023)

The potato famine is a sad story but also one of eventual triumph, and Ireland today has recovered into a beautiful place, filled with beautiful people!

Next, we will look at some of the most famous people that were born there!

Chapter 18: Famous Irish People

Let's look at some of the most famous people that Ireland has provided to the world!

1. Bono was born in Dublin in 1960. He is the lead singer of the legendary rock band U2, which has won more than 20 Grammy awards, making them one of the most-awarded groups in history!

2. Graham Norton was born in Dublin in 1963. He's been the host of his own show on BBC since all the way back in 2007, and interviews some of the biggest stars in the world on it!

3. Rebecca Quin, or "Becky Lynch," was born in Limerick in 1987 and is now one of the World Wrestling Entertainment's biggest stars! She's a multi-time champion and inspires little girls all around the world to follow their dreams!

4. Katie Taylor was born in County Wicklow in 1986. She's a groundbreaking women's boxer who won a gold medal at the 2012 Olympic games, as well as multiple other Olympic medals and world titles!

5. Pierce Brosnan was born in County Meath in 1953. He is a legendary actor who is best known for his role as James Bond, a role that he played for seven years! To many of your parents, Pierce Brosnan *is* James Bond!

6. Bob Geldof might not be a name you recognize, but you'll definitely know all about his legacy! Born in Dublin in 1951, Geldof is best known for creating *Live Aid,* an event that raises money for those without food and water across Africa. Geldof's hard work even saw him knighted by Queen Elizabeth II!

7. Conor McGregor was born in Dublin in 1988. He is one of the most successful mixed martial artists of all time and has been a world champion multiple times!

8. Sonia O'Sullivan was born in Cork in 1969. She is an iconic long-distance runner who was so successful that she raised the profile of Irish sports all on her own. She won a gold medal in 1995, the European championships in 1998, and a silver medal at the Summer Olympics in the year 2000!

9. Niall Horan was born in Mullingar in 1993. He is one of the members of the band One Direction which is one of the best-selling bands of all time and a global icon!

10. Brendan Gleeson is a legendary actor born in Dublin in 1955. He is a Golden Globe nominee and has performed lots of exciting roles, but you probably know him best as Mad Eye Moody from *Harry Potter*!

(*The Most Famous Person From Every County of Ireland,* 2023; O'Hara, 2023a)

Who knew Ireland was the birthplace of so many famous faces? Well, now, the answer is you!

Our next chapter will take a look at one of the more serious parts of Irish history that shaped their history: the troubles of Northern Ireland.

Chapter 19: The Troubles in Northern Ireland

This chapter will look at some of the history behind the division between the Republic of Ireland and Northern Ireland!

1. The troubles in Northern Ireland are sometimes called the Northern Ireland conflict.

2. The division between Northern Ireland and the Republic of Ireland took place in 1920.

3. In the late 1960s, conflict started between the two divided parts of Ireland because Northern Ireland wanted to stay part of the United Kingdom and the Republic of Ireland wanted to create a United Ireland.

4. Another big issue taking place was that those who were Catholic felt they were being treated differently because of

their beliefs. This caused fighting between two different religious groups: the Catholics and the Protestants.

5. The Good Friday Agreement, also known as the Belfast Agreement, was signed in 1998 and saw both sides agree to stop fighting.

6. Sadly, before that agreement was signed, over 3,500 people had lost their lives fighting for what they believed in and more than another 45,000 had been injured.

7. The troubles were so violent and damaging, and every single day of the year marks the anniversary of a death because of them.

8. The British government sent troops to Northern Ireland in the 1970s, hoping that they would be able to bring peace. The troubles ended up continuing for so long that the British stayed there until 2007!

9. The Irish Republican Army (IRA) was a group formed to drive British soldiers out of Northern Ireland and to unite the north of the country with the rest of it.

10. In 2020, a dual government was formed in Ireland, meaning that all parties of the conflict could work towards a better future for the country.

(*The Troubles Facts for Kids*, n.d.; *Belfast Agreement Facts for Kids*, n.d.; *Fact Sheet on the Conflict in and About Northern Ireland*, 2007)

Peace should always be the answer, no matter the conflict!

Next, we'll lighten things back up by looking at some Irish holidays and festivals that aren't Saint Patrick's Day!

Chapter 20: Irish Festivals and Holidays

There's much more to Ireland's festivals and holidays than just St. Patrick's Day! Let's learn about some of the others!

1. Shrove Tuesday is celebrated on the Tuesday before the beginning of Lent. Before Lenten fasting begins pancakes are flipped and eaten all across Ireland—yum!

2. Saint Stephen's Day, or Wren Day, takes place on the 26th of December. Ireland's southern counties celebrate by dressing up in costumes made of straw and singing and dancing for gathered audiences, who donate food, drink, and money!

3. Beltane was a day of celebration in ancient Ireland, celebrated on the 1st of May to mark the start of summer. Bonfires were

once lit all over Ireland, and gatherings were held, but celebrations now tend to be much smaller.

4. Samhain, or Halloween, is celebrated on the 31st of October, and it's a big deal in Ireland because they invented it! The Irish brought the Halloween traditions that we now know and love to America in the 19th century!

5. Good Friday takes place in late March or early April and is dedicated to fasting in honor of the death of Jesus Christ. Hot cross buns, which have a cross of icing across their tops, are eaten, and banks and pubs are usually closed out of respect!

6. Saint Brigid's Day is an annual feast that takes place on or around the 1st of February and marks the beginning of spring. Saint Brigid was one of the three patron saints of Ireland, and the day is now used as an opportunity to celebrate the impact that women have had on Irish history!

7. The Ould Lammas Fair takes place in the town of Ballycastle on the Antrim coast on the last Monday and Tuesday of every year. It sees Ballycastle taken over by a traditional cattle and horse market and includes traditional music that plays throughout the night!

8. The Puck Fair is one of Ireland's oldest and it's quirky and great fun, too! It takes place between the 10th and 12th of August in the town of Killorglin. The town is ruled by a goat, which is celebrated within the town's center. The fair features music, food, and games!

9. The Beo Festival is a music festival that takes place in Dublin in August. It celebrates Celtic culture and traditional Irish music. It includes not only Irish music stars but some of the biggest stars from around the world, too!

10. Every year in Ireland, one lucky town or city hosts the Fleadh Cheoil, which translates as "festival of music." This Irish festival is a little different from others, as it doesn't just include music but competition, with musical acts competing to perform there and winners in various categories being crowned there!

(Irish Holidays You Should Know About, 2022; *Ceili Feiles and Fleadh Traditional Irish Festivals*, n.d.)

Doesn't Ireland sound like a fun place? They love a party!

Next, we're going to learn some facts about some of Ireland's most amazing zoos and wildlife parks!

Chapter 21: Ireland's Zoos and Wildlife Parks

Let's learn about some of Ireland's animal sanctuaries that have been built to protect their precious wildlife and nature!

1. Dublin Zoo first opened in 1831. It was built on just 4 acres of land and started with 72 birds and 46 mammals.

2. Today, Dublin Zoo covers a massive 28 hectares of land! It's the biggest family attraction in Ireland and welcomes over 1 million visitors every year!

3. Fota Wildlife Park can be found in Cork and covers more than 100 acres, where over 70 species of animals call home!

4. Fota Wildlife Park offers overnight stays in lodges, meaning the guests can wake up to the sound of the animals right outside—which sounds absolutely magical!

5. County Cork is home to a donkey sanctuary that has taken in donkeys that have been abandoned or neglected. It's home to more than 1,700 friendly donkeys and mules just waiting to be petted!

6. The National Reptile Zoo in County Kilkenny is home to Ireland's biggest snake—it's over 16 feet long! (So, I guess Saint Patrick didn't drive them all out!)

7. The Killarney National Park is set within the mountainous lands of County Kerry and is packed with beautiful red deer!

8. The Burren Birds of Prey Centre in Clare is home to one of the biggest and most varied collections of birds in the country, including hawks, vultures, and eagles!

9. The Burren National Park is located with the ancient burial sites of the Burren and gives us the chance to see unique and exotic plant life, as well as animals!

10. Tayto Park in County Meath is home to not only more than 300 different animals but also to the biggest wooden roller coaster in all of Europe—that sounds like quite a view!

(*9 Interesting Dublin Zoo Facts*, n.d.; O'Connor, 2021; Licata, 2024)

I think it's safe to say that Ireland is a great destination for animal lovers!

Our next chapter is all about traditional Celtic art and symbols!

Chapter 22: Celtic Art and Symbols

It's time to learn all about Celtic art, symbols, and the meanings behind them!

1. The Celtic Tree of Life is a symbol of a tree with woven branches that represent the human connection to the spiritual realm and deep roots that represent the connection to the ancestral roots of the family!

2. The Celtic cross is a thick cross that represents the Son and the Holy Spirit. It's often used as part of Christian ceremonies (like weddings) as a symbol of faith and hope!

3. The Dara knot is a symbol made of two woven lattice rectangles that represent the union between two people. It's

believed to bring luck, protection, prosperity, and happiness, so it's no surprise that it's a popular necklace design!

4. The Ailm is a symbol made from a plus sign within a thin circle. It represents the cycle of life and is believed to bring protection, luck, health, and happiness. It's also associated with the goddess of fertility, Brigid of the Tuatha de!

5. The Trinity knot, or Triquetra, is a symbol of hope and faith made of three pointed loops that make a triangle. It represents the Holy Trinity (the Father, the Son, and the Holy Spirit) and is believed to bring protection and luck.

6. The Irish harp is a symbol of joy, celebration, and music of course! This symbol of Irish identity is associated with luck, health, and happiness!

7. The Shamrock, or the three-leaf clover, is one of Ireland's most iconic symbols due to its association with Saint Patrick. It represents good fortune, luck, health, happiness, and just about every good omen you would want to follow you around!

8. The Triskelion is a symbol made of three spirals that look like whirlpools, that represent the physical world, spiritual world, and the afterlife. It's also closely linked to the oak tree, which represents courage, protection, resilience, and strength!

9. The Claddagh ring is a traditional Irish ring featuring two hands holding a heart. It represents friendship, love, and loyalty, and it is often passed down through families!

10. The Celtic motherhood knot is a continuous knot that looks similar to a heart and symbolizes the continuous and everlasting love between a mother and her child!

(*12 Celtic Symbols and Meanings Explained*, 2023)

How amazing are those symbols? How many of you are already Googling some of them and seeing how good of a job I did describing them?

Chapter 23 will see us learn a little more about the Titanic, but this time, we're focusing on Belfast's Titanic quarter!

Chapter 23: Belfast's Titanic Quarter

We've learned all about the impact that Ireland had on the creation of the Titanic; now, let's look at Belfast's modern Titanic quarter!

1. Titanic Belfast cost more than an amazing $127 million to construct, making it Northern Ireland's most expensive tourism project ever!

2. The attraction opened for the first time on the 31st of March in 2012, and it had welcomed over half a million visitors after just six months of opening to the public!

3. The attraction's design is very cool and very unique! Three separate buildings are covered in more than 3,000 unique aluminum sheets, none of which are repeated more than 20

times. This creates an amazing landmark that catches the sunlight from all angles like a diamond!

4. The entire building covers more than 150,000 square feet, and its highest point reaches 126.3 feet!

5. The attraction is located just 328 feet away from where the hull of the Titanic was created and launched. Nestled in between the office where it was designed, and the Channel that it first set sail in!

6. The attraction's 10-year anniversary was in 2022, and it was estimated that it had generated over $508 million for Northern Ireland's economy and had welcomed more than 6.5 million visitors from at least 145 different countries!

7. The attraction is home to a rare promotional pamphlet that was designed to encourage people to book tickets for the Titanic's maiden voyage!

8. It's also the only place where you can see an original first-class menu from the ship. The menu was lent to the museum by its owner, a man named Rupert Hunt, who brought it for $122,000!

9. A virtual tour allows you to visit the wreckage of the Titanic on the floor of the Atlantic Ocean—sounds both informative and eerie to me!

10. The Thompson dry dock, where the Titanic once sat, is just feet from the attraction and has been unchanged since the Titanic set sail in 1912!

(*About Titanic Belfast*, n.d.; *Northern Ireland Celebrates Ten Years of a Titanic Impact*, 2022; *Artefacts*, n.d.; *5 Fun Things to See at the Titanic Museum Belfast*, 2020)

As I said, Ireland is really proud of its work in building the Titanic, and it's great to see its economy still benefiting from its hard work after all these years!

We're blasting off into space next, with some facts about Irish contributions to science and space exploration!

Chapter 24: Irish Science and Space Exploration

Let's take a look at some facts about Ireland's contributions to science and space exploration!

1. Agnes Clerke was a woman from the town of Skibbereen whose work on astronomy was so well respected that a crater on the moon was named in her honor!

2. John Tyndall was born in Carlow and holds the honor of being one of the first scientists to understand the greenhouse effect, which is the way that gases trap heat near the Earth's surface!

3. Earnest Walton was an Irish physicist from County Waterford, who was part of the first pair of scientists to successfully split the atom! They were awarded a joint Nobel Prize for their discovery in 1951!

4. Jocelyn Bell Burnell is an astrophysicist from Northern Ireland who discovered the first radio pulsars back in 1967, which helps us find evidence of gravitational radiation! Burnell's work saw her awarded an honorary degree by Dublin City University in 2015!

5. Kenneth Edgeworth was a theoretical astronomer who realized that Pluto wasn't actually a planet. Edgeworth's discovery is very impressive when you realize he made it back in 1938 and Pluto was believed to be a planet up until 2006!

6. Robert Boyle was an Irish philosopher and chemist from the 17th century who invented Boyle's Law. His law explained the relationship between the pressure and volume of gas and inspired Isaac Newton! Amazingly, Boyle also created a list of 24 inventions that he hoped to see in his lifetime and it included electricity and human flight!

7. Norah Patten is an award-winning aeronautical engineer from Ballina, who is set to become the first Irish person to go to space! She was inspired by her first trip to NASA at just 11 years old!

8. John Joly was born in Bracknagh and is best known for his incredible work in recognizing that radiotherapy can treat cancer!

9. Frank Pantridge was a cardiologist and physician from County Down. He established his own cardiology unit at Queen's

University, where he was able to develop the first modern system for CPR!

10. Ellen Hutchins was Ireland's first-ever female botanist, who is someone who studies plants and fungi. After growing up in Ballylickey in 1785, she set to work discovering hundreds of new plants and species!

(*Irish Scientists and Inventors*, n.d.; *13 Exceptional Irish Scientists You Absolutely Need to Know*, 2015; Vaal, 2023)

Where would the worlds of science and space exploration be without Ireland? Luckily, we won't have to find out!

In the next chapter, we're learning all about some of Ireland's most famous landmarks!

Chapter 25: Famous Irish Landmarks

Let's learn all about some of Ireland's most famous landmarks!

1. The Rock of Cashel in Tipperary looks like it's right out of a fairytale! The medieval buildings have been standing since before the fifty century!

2. The Monasterboice High Crosses in County Louth are an incredible trio of Celtic crosses that are accompanied by two 14th-century churches and an ancient round tower that was used to spot approaching enemies!

3. Newgrange in Meath is one of the country's most ancient monuments and dates all the way back to 3200 B.C.E. It's believed that the monument was built by worshippers of a religion based on the stars!

4. The Spire of Dublin is a 393-foot-tall monument that stretches into the sky like a pin. It was built in 2002 after the design was chosen as the winner of a competition to find a replacement for Nelson's Pillar!

5. This brings us to Nelson's Pillar! The Pillar was erected in 1809 and was a 170-foot-tall column with a statue of British flag officer Horatio Nelson. It was sadly blown up by members of the IRA in 1966.

6. Christ Church Cathedral in Dublin was founded back in the 11th century by Sitric Silkenbeard, a Viking king! Unsurprisingly, it's one of Dublin's most popular landmarks!

7. Kylemore Abbey is a castle that was built in 1867 and now serves as a nunnery for Benedictine nuns. Located in Connemara, it includes a neo-gothic church and is one of the most famous Irish landmarks because it makes a great postcard picture!

8. Mizen Head is located in West Cork and is a former fog signal station that offers stunning views of cliffs and the Atlantic Ocean. There is also a bridge to cross them and a mini museum where you can learn about the area's history!

9. Reginald's Tower is a Viking lookout tower that was built in Waterford between 1253 and 1280. Today, it serves as a Viking museum that showcases the rich history of the city!

10. The Derry Walls were originally built between 1613 and 1619 to protect the English and Scottish plantation workers who had moved there. The walls are still standing to this day and are 26 feet high, just slightly under one mile in circumference, and enclose the inner city!

(O'Hara, 2023b; *17th Century City Walls*, n.d.)

How incredible do some of those landmarks sound? I think a trip to Ireland is in order, or at least it will be after our next chapter, which is all about Ireland's stunning coastline and seas!

Chapter 26: Ireland's Coastline and Seas

Let's explore facts about the coastline, including the beaches and seas around them!

1. Ireland is surrounded by not one, not two, but *three* different seas! The West of Ireland is served by the Atlantic Ocean, the Southern side offers views of the Celtic Sea, and the East of Ireland is hit by the waves of the Irish Sea!

2. It's the Irish Sea that separates Ireland from England and the Isle of Man is an island that rests between the two!

3. In fact, the Irish Sea is home to more than 50 individual islands and most of them are populated!

4. Ireland's coastline stretches 4,675 miles and offers an incredible 140 different beaches! The east of Ireland is better known for being rocky and mountainous and the west is known for its sensationally sandy beaches!

5. Portsalon Beach is located in the town of Donegal, and its sandy beaches are so stunning that it was once voted the world's second most beautiful beach!

6. Strandhill Beach in Sligo is a surfer's paradise, thanks to the clean breaks and dramatic swells of the ocean!

7. The Irish Sea connects four major coastal cities—connecting Dublin and Belfast in Ireland to Blackpool and Liverpool in England!

8. The Irish Sea is home to more than 35 different species of fish and the second-largest species of shark, the basking shark, is known to hang out in it, too!

9. There are also a lot of different species of dolphins that live in Irish waters, including Fungi, a famous bottlenose dolphin that delighted Irish people by getting up close to both humans and boats between 1983 and 2020!

10. Puffins are the most beloved marine bird of the Irish coast, and they love to relax on their shores in spring and early summer before spending the rest of the year in Ireland's oceans!

(Carter, 2024; *9 Wee Facts About the Irish Sea*, 2021; Rainbolt, 2021)

Ireland is clearly blessed with some incredible views, seas, and aquatic life! Our next chapter is all about traditional Irish crafts!

Chapter 27: Traditional Irish Crafts

This chapter is all about traditional Irish crafts, let's get creative!

1. Irish lace is typically made with fine thread-like linen or cotton and dates back to the 17th century when Irish women brought the techniques home after learning them abroad. It's usually used to create women's clothing, like blouses and wedding blouses!

2. Aran sweaters were created on the Aran Islands just off the west coast of Ireland and were knit by hand, using the wool from the Island's sheep! It was often the wives of the fishermen who made the sweaters in order to keep their husbands nice and toasty while they were out on their boats!

3. Celtic jewelry dates back to ancient times and is known for having fancy, intricate designs made from knots, spirals, and interwoven lace. It also holds symbolic meaning relating to the cycle of life!

4. Irish pottery dates back hundreds and hundreds of years to the New Stone Age. During that time, pottery wasn't made to look nice—it was all about function. But over time, nice patterns that included flowers, leaves, and shells were added. Today, Irish pottery is both functional and beautifully designed, usually including the Celtic symbols we explored earlier on!

5. Tweed is a rough woolen fabric that is known for being tough! The need for tough clothes to protect them against the elements saw the Irish hand-weave tweed into clothes that could protect them against the harsh weather. Today, tweed jackets are an absolute staple of traditional Irish outfits and are usually paired with a tweed hat, too!

6. Bodhran drums were made back in ancient Celtic times so that they could be played at gatherings and celebrations. They were made by stretching goat skin tightly over a wooden frame and pinning it down!

7. Ireland has a long history with the beautiful stained glass that you can see on Church windows, and it all started when churches were built around the country during the early Christian period!

8. Connemara marble is a green marble that can only be found in the Connemara region of West Ireland. For centuries, Irish people have used saws, chisels, and grinders to carve that unique marble into beautiful jewelry!

9. Ireland has a rich history of woodwork, with the country's timber turned into stunning furniture such as tables and chairs using hand tools like carving knives and saws. Traditional Irish woodwork usually features Celtic patterns or symbols of nature, like trees!

10. Basket making and willow weaving is an Irish tradition that goes back centuries, with baskets made from willow rods!

(Augello, 2023; 5 *Traditional Crafts of Ireland*, 2020)

Who fancies doing some arts and crafts then?

Next, we're going to learn some facts specifically about one of Ireland's most unique landmarks: the Burren!

Chapter 28: The Burren

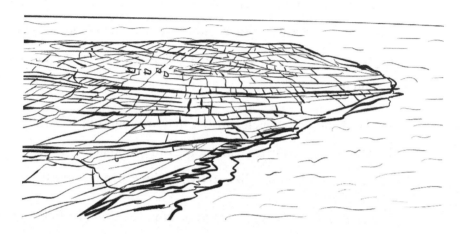

Let's look at some facts about the Burren, Ireland's unique limestone landscape!

1. The Burren is a landscape made entirely of limestone, that covers 135 square miles, which is roughly 0.5% of the whole of Ireland!

2. The limestone took over 20 million years to form and is made up of the fossilized organisms of marine life!

3. In some places, the limestone that makes up the Burren is as thick as 2,559 feet!

4. Some of the oldest rocks found on the Burren's surface are tens of millions of years old!

5. The Aran Islands were formed when they broke away from the Burren at the end of the last Ice Age!

6. Even though it looks pretty bare, the Burren is actually packed with life! More than 1,100 plant species call it home and the combination of plants that grow together is unique! Plants that usually need warm weather and those that need cold are able to grow right next to each other because of how unique the ground is!

7. Seven of the nine species of bat that are found in Ireland are found in the Burren, including the endangered Lesser Horseshoe Bats, which like to live in the Burren's caves!

8. The Burren Hills are believed to be home to around 1,000 feral goats!

9. The unique limestone rock of the Burren contains calcium carbonate, which is great for helping snails strengthen their shells. This might explain why more than 70 species of land snail call it home!

10. Ireland is home to a total of 27 wild orchids and 23 of them are found in the Burren. These include the wildflower dropwort, *Filipendula vulgaris*, which doesn't grow anywhere else in the country!

11. The Burren looks a little like the Moon due to its color and rocky landscape, which is probably why its name, "Burren," means "rocky area!"

(Kirby, 2016; *The Geology of the Burren*, 2013; *Flora and Fauna*, 2013)

Doesn't the Burren sound amazing?!

Our next chapter will take a bit of a left turn and focus on facts about the Irish education system!

Chapter 29: Irish Education

Next up are facts all about Ireland's schools and learning!

1. Between the ages of 6 and 16, education in Ireland is compulsory (meaning you have to go!), but luckily, completely free!

2. English is the main language taught in Irish schools, with Irish taught as a second language. But there are also "Gaelscoileanna" schools, which teach Irish as their main language and English as a foreign one!

3. All college and university courses are in English as it's Ireland's first language, this also makes the country an attractive prospect international students!

4. Some schools in Ireland are small—really small. There are a total of 3,250 primary (elementary) schools, and 200 of them have just 2 teachers, with another 200 having just 3 or 4 teachers, too!

5. Most Irish children start school at just 4 years old, with most primary schools offering infant classes!

6. The school year in Ireland runs from September to June, and in lots of schools the day starts at 8:30 a.m. and ends at 4:30 p.m.!

7. There are three tiers in the Irish education system: primary (elementary), secondary (high school), and the third level (university) and further education.

8. Historically, Irish schools have had strong ties to the Catholic Church, with many schools being run by religious orders. However, there are also non-denominational and multi-denominational schools.

9. In Ireland, some bachelor's degrees based on job-oriented subjects are free to Irish, United Kingdom (UK), European Union (EU), and Swiss students! International students applying for a course that isn't free can apply for bursaries and scholarships!

10. The country also offers a very helpful post-study visa for international students who have studied in the country! It's all

part of improving the job market for Ireland and making sure they get the most talented workers!

(kevmrc, 2023; *8 Facts about Study in Ireland*, 2022)

The Irish education system is clearly focused on giving children the best chance at reaching their potential so that they can benefit the country, as well as inviting the best from other countries, too!

Personally, I love their approach!

Our next chapter is all about the way that Ireland is represented in pop culture!

Chapter 30: Ireland in Pop Culture

Let's learn some facts about Ireland in pop culture, including movies and television shows!

1. Belfast was a huge hub for the cast and crew of *Game of Thrones* and areas across Ireland were used for some of the show's most iconic moments. Including the Carrick-a-Rede rope bridge in Ballintoy and the Cushendun Caves in Ballymena!

2. The iconic horcrux cave in *Harry Potter and the Half-Blood Prince* was actually filmed at the Cliffs of Moher in County Clare!

3. The magical comedy *The Princess Bride* also used the Cliffs of Moher as a filming location, both for an epic sword fight and as a location in the film called The Cliffs of Insanity!

4. Ireland's beauty was also used as a stunning location for *Star Wars: The Force Awakens*. During the reconstruction of the Millennium Falcon, which was filmed in Malin Head, Donegal, and Skellig Michael, an island in County Kerry, was used for the location that Luke Skywalker was hiding out in when Rey went to find him!

5. *The Lord of the Rings* was said to be heavily influenced by some of Ireland's beautiful landscapes. The franchise's roots in Ireland run so deep that festivals held in the Burren are believed to have inspired J. R. R. Tolkien to write the books!

6. *Derry Girls* is a television show that wasn't just filmed in Northern Ireland but the story follows teenage girls growing up in Derry during the troubles of Northern Ireland!

7. Unsurprisingly given the country's roots, the television show *Vikings* has filmed all over it, including the lakes and mountains of County Wicklow, Nun's beach in County Kerry, and the River Boyne in County Meath!

8. The animated movie *The Book of Kells* tells the story of a young apprentice of a local monastery using the power and magic of the book to repel a Viking attack!

9. *The Luck of the Irish* is a Disney movie about a high school student who realizes that he's part leprechaun after losing his pot-of-gold charm and has to find the thief who stole it before they use the leprechauns for evil!

10. *Sing Street* is a movie set in Dublin in the 1980s and is all about a boy who is transferred from a private school to a tougher inner-city one. Once he's there, he starts a band with the students who he thought he had nothing in common with—it's a great introduction to the traditional Irish music of the '80s!

(*Ireland's Most Recognizable Sites in Pop Culture and Films*, n.d.; *Where in Ireland Is Vikings Filmed*, 2021; Manning, 2021)

It's no surprise that Ireland has been such a popular source of stories and locations, given its history and beauty!

The next chapter is all about Ireland's most beautiful geographical features!

Chapter 31: Irish Geography

Let's learn some facts about Ireland's rivers, mountains, and other beautiful geographical features!

1. Ireland is home to more than 3,100 rivers!

2. The largest river in Ireland is the River Shannon. It's over 224 miles long and begins at the Spring of Shannon in County Cavan before emptying into the Atlantic Ocean at the Shannon Estuary in Limerick!

3. The River Shannon is seen as the divider of the country because it flows through 11 counties and splits the east and south of the country away from the west. There are only a total of 20 different crossings along the whole of the river!

4. The River Suir, River Noir, and River Barrow all join the Celtic Sea from the Southeast bay in Waterford and are called "the Three Sisters." The trio don't all share the same starting point, though. The River Barrow starts in the Slieve Bloom Mountains of County Laois and the River Nore and Suir start in County Tipperary!

5. Small streams are really important to Ireland's ecosystem, and they make up 77% of the length of the Irish river network!

6. There are 31 total mountain ranges across Ireland!

7. The highest mountain in Ireland is Carrauntoohil, which is found in County Kerry. It's part of the MacGillycuddy's Reeks Mountain range and has a peak of 3,405 feet!

8. Mount Brandon is a mountain also found in County Kerry that peaks at 3,116 feet tall. It's named after the Irish Saint Brendan and forms part of a famous Christian pilgrimage route!

9. Slieve Donard in County Down is Northern Ireland's tallest mountain and peaks at 2,788 feet! It's part of the Mourne Mountains and is very popular with tourists!

10. Mangerton in County Kerry peaks at 2,749 feet. Although it might not be as high as some of the others in this chapter, it's home to the Horse's Glen, which is a U-shaped valley that runs along the beautiful Devil's Punchbowl Lake!

(*What Are the Rivers of Ireland?*, n.d.; *The Importance of the Small Stream Network in Ireland*, 2019; Badnjarevic, 2020)

Isn't Ireland filled with beautiful natural wonders?

Next, we'll learn all about some of the secrets behind Ireland's ancient ruins!

Chapter 32: Ireland's Ancient Ruins

Let's explore some of the mysteries of Ireland's ancient ruins!

1. The Hill of Tara is a limestone ridge found in County Meath. It's a Stone Age burial site that once served as the headquarters of Celtic kings!

2. In Newgrange, County Meath, there are three Neolithic burial mounds that are older than the Egyptian pyramids!

3. The monastic sites of Glendalough in County Wicklow date back to the 11th century. The site includes St Kevin's Church, which goes even further back to the 6th century. And the ruins of churches, round towers, and stone crosses are still standing today!

4. The heritage sites of Skellig Michael are found on a barren rocky island off the coast of Kerry. They date all the way back to 800 and were once a tiny monastery made of oratories (places of worship), six beehive huts, and a little garden!

5. The ancient monuments of Clonmacnoise are found within a bend of the River Shannon near Athlone. It's the country's biggest monastic site and served as an important waterway in 545. The site includes the ruins of stone graves, two round towers, three high crosses, a cathedral, and seven churches!

6. In Ireland's northwest, you'll find Carrowmore megalithic cemetery. The cemetery is from the Bronze Age, making it over 6,000 years old. It's the biggest cemetery of its kind in the country and has over 35 stone grave sites!

7. There are stone circles in both Kerry and West Cork that have upright pillars on either side of a burial site. These sites were used for rituals involving the sun and the biggest in the country, the Drombeg stone circle, is made of 17 stones! Drombeg isn't just the biggest of these circles—it's also the most complete of the Bronze Age remains found in the country and dates all the way back to 1124–794 B.C.E.!

8. The Ardmore Cathedral and Round Tower, found in County Waterford, are the ruins of a cathedral that dates back to the 12th century. What's left of them stands proudly on a clifftop—how's that for a view?!

9. The abbey ruins on Innisfallen Island date all the way back to the 7th century and are said to have been the place where monks educated Brian Boru, the last High King of Ireland. Here's a cool bonus for you: The ruins can only be reached by row boat!

10. The 5th-century ruins of Dunseverick Castle are found on the Causeway coastline, which once served as the home of ancient leaders, tribal groups, and Irish royalty!

(Sarah, 2023; *Dunseverick Castle*, n.d.)

Ireland has an incredibly rich history, and the ancient ruins tell incredible chapters of its story!

Next, we'll learn some facts about the truly stunning, Wild Atlantic Way!

Chapter 33: The Wild Atlantic Way

This chapter will take you along Ireland's stunning west coast!

1. The Wild Atlantic Way is a tourism trail that starts in Malin Head in County Donegal and ends in Kinsale in County Cork. It stretches along 1,553 miles, passing through nine counties and three provinces!

2. The Wild Atlantic Way features Europe's highest sea cliffs at Slieve League in County Donegal!

3. Waves reach as high as 29 to 39 feet just off the coast of Sligo, making it a great spot for surfers and for people who want to watch those surfers tackle huge waves!

4. The Kerry International Dark Sky Reserve is so rural and lacks natural light that the stars in the night sky are incredibly bright on clear nights!

5. The Wild Atlantic Way features 30 stunning islands, from the Aran Islands, which feel like stepping back in time to ancient Ireland, to the beautiful paradise of Achill Island. Dursey Island in Cork is home to the only cable car in the country, too—each island is like its own little world!

6. Serpent's Lair is found in Inishmore just off the Galway coast and offers a stomach-churning 92-foot dive into the water below!

7. The stunning village of Annascaul in County Kerry was the birthplace of a legendary seaman named Tom Crean, who was a member of three incredible expeditions to the Antarctic between 1900 and 1917! Today, the village has an exhibition dedicated to Crean's adventures!

8. The largest island in Ireland, Achill Island, is home to a village known only as "deserted village," and no one knows why it was abandoned in the early 20th century—spooky!

9. The route of the Wild Atlantic Way was launched in 2014. It's divided into five sections:

   - County Donegal

   - County Donegal to County Mayo

   - County Mayo to County Clare

- County Clare to County Kerry

- County Kerry to County Cork

10. It features a total of 157 discovery points, 1,000 attractions, and over 2,500 activities to do!

(*Ten Fantastic Facts About the Wild Atlantic Way*, n.d.; *Wild Atlantic Way Facts for Kids*, n.d.)

The Wild Atlantic Way is a truly stunning way to see the Emerald Isle, and is the type of trip that everyone should try and do at least once in their lives!

Next, we'll learn some facts about the Irish lighthouses that have been lighting the way for the likes of Tom Crean!

Chapter 34: Irish Lighthouses

Our last chapter will take a look at some of the Irish lighthouses that have guided ships for centuries!

1. There are a total of 70 lighthouses that are still keeping sailors coming in and out of Ireland safe!

2. The Hook Head lighthouse in County Wexford is nearly 800 years old (making it the oldest working lighthouse in Ireland). It was built in the 13th century by a knight named William Marshal, who was believed to be the greatest knight ever! He built the house to protect trade ships.

3. Hook Head has been electrically operated since 1972 and has been able to operate automatically since 1996!

4. Before Marshal built the lighthouse, it was the job of 5th-century monks to keep sailors safe, which they did by keeping a bonfire alight!

5. Ballycotton Lighthouse was built in the late 1840s, and you can only reach it by boat. This made getting to school really difficult for the children who lived in it with their families until 1896!

6. Mizen Head Lighthouse in County Cork lies at Ireland's most southerly point. In 1908, it was the scene of a shipwreck that saw the lighthouse engineer and staff incredibly save 68 lives!

7. The Fanad Lighthouse was built in 1817 as the result of a shipwreck, but it has sadly seen not one but two tragic shipwrecks! In 1915, its keepers witnessed the sinking of an ocean liner during World War I, and two years later, a ship called the SS *Laurentic* sank nearby. When the SS *Laurentic* sank, the gold bars on board sank to the bottom of the ocean, and there are 22 gold bars that haven't been found yet!

8. Rathlin West Light, in County Antrim, Northern Ireland, is a lighthouse with a difference. It's the only lighthouse in the country that's upside down!

9. Valentia Island Lighthouse was built in 1837 and sits within the site of a 17th-century fort that was built to protect the Valentia Harbor.

10. The rocky shore near the Valentia Island Lighthouse is imprinted with the fossilized footprint of a dinosaur!

11. The tallest lighthouse that Ireland has to offer is Fastnet Lighthouse, which is found on the Fastnet Rock in the Atlantic Ocean and stretches as tall as 177 feet into the air!

(*Hook Lighthouse: 5 Things You Didn't Know*, n.d.; *Fantastic Lighthouse Facts*, n.d.; *Ireland's Lighthouses*, 2020)

Isn't it amazing to think that before lighthouses existed, monks were lighting the way with bonfires and burning braziers?

That does it for our lighthouse facts, and indeed our Ireland facts! I'll see you for the conclusion to wrap things up!

A Quick Pause...

If this book has helped you in any way, we'd appreciate it if you left us a review on Amazon. Reviews are the lifeblood of our business. We read every single one and incorporate your feedback into our future book projects.

To leave an Amazon review please visit https://www.amazon.com/ryp or scan the QR code below...THANK YOU!

Chapter 35: Worksheets and Puzzles

Find Ireland and Northern Ireland

- Find Ireland and Northern Ireland on the map of Europe and shade them in.
- The capital city of Ireland is _____ .
- The capital city of Northern Ireland is _____ .
- Indicate the capitals' locations on the map.

Ireland Fact File

Official name of the country:

_____

Main city:

_____

Language spoken:

_____

What the people are called:

_____

Money used:

_____

Religion followed:

_____

Size of the country:

_____

Number of people:

_____

Biggest city:

_____

Leader:

_____

National holiday:

_____

Where it is in the world:

_____

Color the flag with the right colors.

Find and mark the capital on the map.

Find Ireland on the map below.

Color by County – Ireland

Cork	Derry	Antrim	Wexford	Wicklow	Westmeath	Fermanagh	Longford
Galway	Tipperary	Limerick	Meath	Offaly	Sligo	Leitrim	Dublin
Mayo	Clare	Roscommon	Kerry	Cavan	Laois	Armagh	Carlow
Donegal	Tyrone	Down	Kilkenny	Waterford	. Kildare	Monaghan	Louth

Name the County – Ireland

Find the counties Ireland and Northern Ireland
and write it in the correct space.

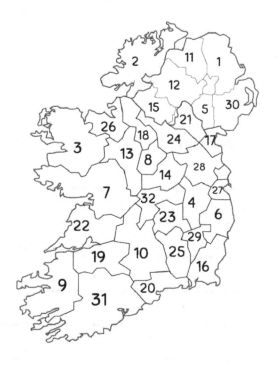

1. _____	8. _____	15. _____	22. _____	29. _____
2. _____	9. _____	16. _____	23. _____	30. _____
3. _____	10. _____	17. _____	24. _____	31. _____
4. _____	11. _____	18. _____	25. _____	32. _____
5. _____	12. _____	19. _____	26. _____	
6. _____	13. _____	20. _____	27. _____	
7. _____	14. _____	21. _____	28. _____	

Complete the County Towns by Province

Use this worksheet to find the towns of each province and write them in the blank spaces

In the past, Ireland was divided into Ulster, Connacht, Leinster, Munster, and Meath provinces. Presently, only four provinces are still recognized. King John of England played a role in subdividing Ireland's provinces into counties, and today, each county and province has its own unique cultural heritage and identity.

ULSTER	MUNSTER	LEINSTER	CONNACHT
B_____	E_____	C_____	G_____
A_____	C_____	D_____	C_____
C_____	T_____	N_____	S_____
D_____	L_____	K_____	R_____
L_____	C_____	P_____	S_____
D_____	N_____	L_____	C_____
E_____	W_____	D_____	
M_____		N_____	
O_____		T_____	
		M_____	
		W_____	
		W_____	

Create a Costume for Your
Halloween Celebrations

Use the space provided below to carefully plan and design your Halloween costume. Think about all the details you want to include and how you want your costume to look.

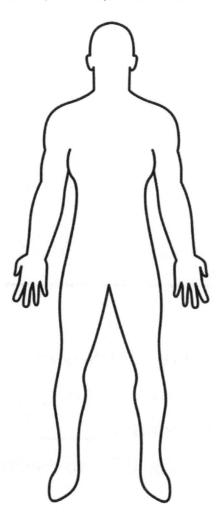

My Halloween Costume

Draw a picture of yourself in a Halloween costume and the scene around you.

1. In this picture, I am dressed as _____

2. For my costume, I put on _____

3. The background is _____

4. Next year I would like to dress as _____

My Perfect Halloween

• What do you like to dress up as on Halloween night?

_____

• Can you name three spooky creatures often associated with Halloween?

_____

• What is the purpose of carving a pumpkin on Halloween?

_____

• How do you feel when you walk through a haunted house?

_____

• Do you prefer trick-or-treating in your neighborhood or at a mall? Why?

_____

• What's your favorite Halloween candy or treat to get while trick-or-treating?

_____

• If you could design your own haunted house, what spooky features would you include?

_____

• What's the scariest costume you've ever seen on Halloween?

_____

• Can you name three famous Halloween movies or TV shows?

_____

• What safety rules should you follow while trick-or-treating on Halloween night?

_____

Create Your Own Haunted House

Use the space below to design your own haunted house for Halloween.

What Haunts Your House?

Write down all the spooky things you would have in your haunted house.

_____
_____
_____
_____

Draw the items from your list in the rooms of your haunted house and label them.

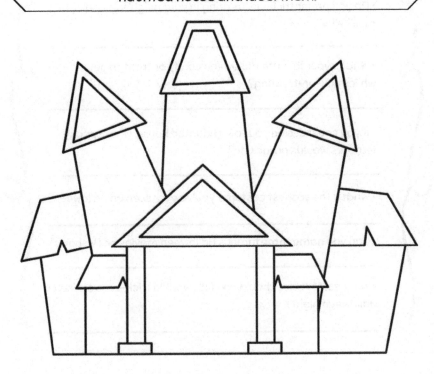

Reasons to Visit Ireland

I think I should visit Ireland because of the following reasons:

Topic Sentence:
I think my teacher should be _____
for Halloween.

Reason #1: _____

_____

Explanation: _____

_____

Reason #2: _____

_____

Explanation: _____

_____

Reason #3: _____

_____

Explanation: _____

_____

Concluding Sentence: _____

_____

Ireland A–Z

Name one Irish-related word for each letter of the alphabet.

A. _____   N. _____

B. _____   O. _____

C. _____   P. _____

D. _____   Q. _____

E. _____   R. _____

F. _____   S. _____

G. _____   T. _____

H. _____   U. _____

I. _____   V. _____

J. _____   W. _____

K. _____   X. _____

L. _____   Y. _____

M. _____   Z. _____

Unscramble the Words

Unscramble the Irish Landmarks.

1. mheor hsiffCl oM _____

2. nGiatss sCuaae _____

3. udDin alestC _____

4. rliyitT Cglolee, ublDin _____

5. yranBel tslaCe _____

6. gniR fo ryKae _____

7. kcoR fo lelsaCh _____

8. ewnNargge _____

9. Sgkleli cMheiarl _____

10. heT nreBu _____

11. reeymKlo ybKa _____

12. nioColmnaocls _____

13. ldeahiMa saCtel _____

14. uceDln aslCte _____

15. rtiSk.Picartr 'ls sthleeadC, unlbDi _____

Navigating the Saint Patrick's Day Maze

Guide St. Patrick through the twists and turns of the maze to find his way to the shamrock. Can you help him navigate the path and reach the lucky shamrock at the end? Use your skills to solve the maze and ensure St. Patrick finds his way!

Pot of Gold Maze

Find your way through the maze to the pot of gold.

Clover Path Puzzle

Assist St. Patrick in navigating the tricky Clover Path Puzzle to uncover the coveted pot of gold awaiting at its ending.

Create your own leprechaun and design their home.

Draw somewhere to live for your leprechaun

Create your personalized Gaelic football jersey.

Select a Gaelic football team and craft their home jersey for the forthcoming season.

Presidents of Ireland Since 1938–Present

Name	Term of office	
	25 June 1938	24 June 1945
	25 June 1945	24 June 1959
	25 June 1959	24 June 1973
	25 June 1973	17 November 1974
	19 December 1974	22 October 1976
	3 December 1976	2 December 1990
	3 December 1990	12 September 1997
	11 November 1997	10 November 2011
	11 November 2011	Present

The New President

Name of the new President

_____

The first action I would take as President
is _____

_____

Who would you choose as your Vice
President and why?

_____

What would your daily activities be? _____

_____

_____

How would you improve the country?_____

_____

_____

What would be the most rewarding aspect of being President?

_____

_____

What would be the most challenging part _____

_____

_____

Color the Irish flag

Green　　　White　　　Orange

Color the Irish flag with Liam

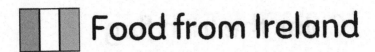 # Food from Ireland

What types of food are eaten in Ireland?

_____

_____

_____

_____

Draw a common meal eaten in the Ireland.

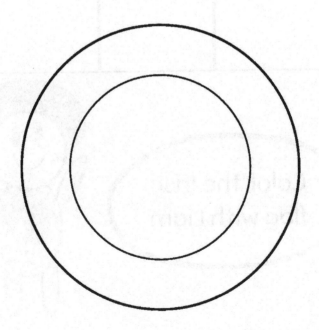

Ireland Travel Brochure

A famous magazine has asked you to write some content for their small travel brochure to encourage people to visit Ireland. Choose a destination or landmark, write an eye-catching headline, give facts and information about the place, and include a picture that illustrates its beauty.

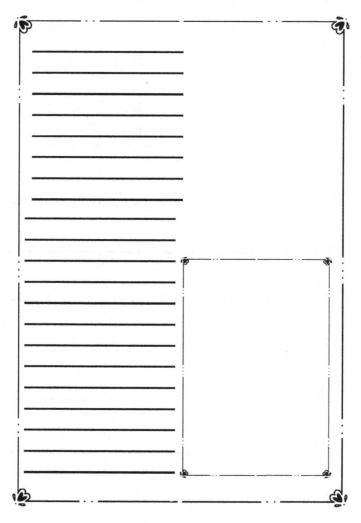

What Have You Learned About Ireland?

I   _____

R   _____

E   _____

L   _____

A   _____

N   _____

D   _____

Color by County – Ireland

Answer Sheet

1. Antrim	5. Armagh	9. Kerry	13. Roscommon	17. Louth	21. Monaghan	25. Kilkenny	29. Carlow
2. Donegal	6. Wicklow	10. Tipperary	14. Westmeath	18. Leitrim	22. Clare	26. Sligo	30. Down
3. Mayo	7. Galway	11. Derry	15. Fermanagh	19. Limerick	23. Laois	27. Dublin	31. Cork
4. Kildare	8. Longford	12. Tyrone	16. Wexford	20. Waterford	24. Cavan	28. Meath	32. Offaly

Name the County – Ireland

1. Antrim	8. Longford	15. Fermanagh	22. Clare	29. Carlow
2. Donegal	9. Kerry	16. Wexford	23. Laois	30. Down
3. Mayo	10. Tipperary	17. Louth	24. Cavan	31. Cork
4. Kildare	11. Derry	18. Leitrim	25. Kilkenny	32. Offaly
5. Armagh	12. Tyrone	19. Limerick	26. Sligo	
6. Wicklow	13. Roscommon	20. Waterford	27. Dublin	
7. Galway	14. Westmeath	21. Monaghan	28. Meath	

Complete the County Towns by Province

Use this worksheet to find the towns of each province and write them in the blank spaces

In the past, Ireland was divided into Ulster, Connacht, Leinster, Munster, and Meath provinces. Presently, only four provinces are still recognized. King John of England played a role in subdividing Ireland's provinces into counties, and today, each county and province has its own unique cultural heritage and identity.

ULSTER	MUNSTER	LEINSTER	CONNACHT
Belfast	Ennis	Carlow	Galway
Armagh	Cork	Dublin	Carrick-on-
Cavan	Tralee	Naas	Shannon
Derry	Limerick	Kilkenny	Roscommon
Lifford	Clonmel	Portlaois	Sligo
Dawnpatrick	Nenagh	Longford	Castlebar
Enniskillen	Waterford	Dundalk	
Monaghan		Navan	
Omagh		Tullamore	
		Mullingar	
		Wexford	
		Wicklow	

Unscramble the Words
Unscramble the Irish Landmarks.

1. Cliffs of Moher

2. Giants Causeway

3. Dublin Castle

4. Trinity College, Dublin

5. Blarney Castle

6. Ring of Kerry

7. Rock of Cashel

8. Newgrange

9. Skellig Michael

10. The Burren

11. Kylemore Abbey

12. Clonmacnoise

13. Malahide Castle

14. Dunluce Castle

15. St. Patrick's Cathedral, Dublin

Navigating the Saint Patrick's Day Maze

Guide St. Patrick through the twists and turns of the maze to find his way to the shamrock. Can you help him navigate the path and reach the lucky shamrock at the end? Use your skills to solve the maze and ensure St. Patrick finds his way!

Pot of Gold Maze

Find your way through the maze to the pot of gold.

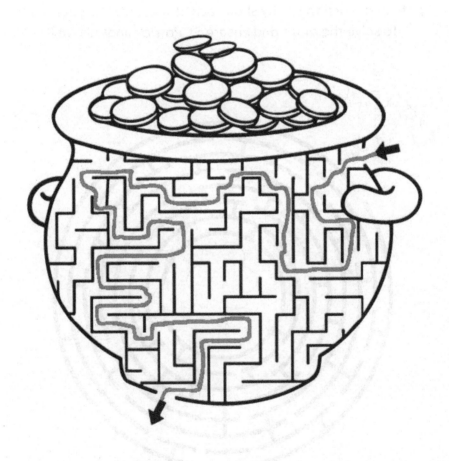

140

Clover Path Puzzle

Assist St. Patrick in navigating the tricky Clover Path Puzzle to uncover the coveted pot of gold awaiting at its ending.

Presidents of Ireland Since 1938–Present

Name	Term of office	
Douglas Hyde	25 June 1938	24 June 1945
Seán T. O'Kelly	25 June 1945	24 June 1959
Éamon de Valera	25 June 1959	24 June 1973
Erskine H. Childers	25 June 1973	17 November 1974
Cearbhall Ó Dálaigh	19 December 1974	22 October 1976
Patrick Hillery	3 December 1976	2 December 1990
Mary Robinson	3 December 1990	12 September 1997
Mary McAleese	11 November 1997	10 November 2011
Michael D. Higgins	11 November 2011	Present

HISTORY

```
R I L Y L L I T E R A T U R E A Z
H Y V G Y J E Y F C R E T S A E Y
I Q K D L Y S L L E W M O R C M O
N D B C Y S N R X V I K I N G S C
X O X P I T M O N A S T E R I E S
U O R F L R B V I A C D U K L P S
X A P M Z A T I R L N J T T F J H
H B D S A Y N A Z E L Y S A F I O
B M A L N N T T P P B E M E G M F
Q U E B T F S E A T Z I B H L I S
L L R D O C D C P T N Z K E O K D
X O O L I N Q I B E I I W E R Y I
N C L P I E C L H Z N O A X D I U
F I K Z T C V E X G Q W N S S K R
H E L M W Z E A S U B C E S H I D
S B O J L R A G L M S G T K I Q U
M T F P I S U F V T L C P D P W R
```

CELTS	FAMINE	EASTER
GAELIC	DRUIDS	VIKINGS
NORMANS	COLUMBA	CROMWELL
FOLKLORE	MEDIEVAL	LORDSHIP
REBELLION	LITERATURE	HIGH KINGS
MONASTERIES	PLANTATIONS	INDEPENDENCE
HILL OF TARA	SAINT PATRICK	

▮▮ IRISH LOCATIONS

```
O V N A H G A N O M Y V S Y
W I K M G A L W A Y W O S T
O M I B K D F A K H O N R H
S R N L J C P T I H L A A A
E N N I S O I E L N L V E U
A E E U K R M R K E A A R D
Q H G W K K N F E O M N H U
D G A O B Y F O N M N E G N
U A D L X R B R N V I S U D
B N Y R Y Z I D Y M L L O A
L E R A J X X D X I R E L L
I N R C A D E H G O R D T K
N B G Q U C S O Q E E J F S
Y A W Z G K H U T A H W X D
```

CORK	BRAY	SLIGO
NAVAN	ENNIS	DUBLIN
GALWAY	CARLOW	TRALEE
MALLOW	NENAGH	DUNDALK
LIMERICK	DROGHEDA	KILKENNY
KINNEGAD	LOUGHREA	MONAGHAN
WATERFORD	NEWBRIDGE	

IRISH LOCATIONS 2

```
K  L  R  J  E  G  D  I  R  B  L  E  C  U  A  M  S
A  N  A  R  C  N  U  B  E  U  C  M  H  Y  M  T  K
G  G  G  C  A  E  N  V  Y  D  R  O  F  X  E  W  C
W  B  N  O  U  I  S  W  E  U  I  P  C  O  U  D  L
E  Y  I  B  C  O  H  I  N  N  S  H  R  U  S  H  O
Q  J  L  H  L  S  A  C  O  G  D  P  A  Z  J  B  N
Y  R  L  C  A  R  U  K  L  A  C  V  R  L  A  G  M
S  P  U  N  R  G  G  L  H  R  L  H  R  L  A  C  E
A  R  M  I  E  R  H  O  T  V  J  T  B  L  V  M  L
I  M  B  D  G  E  L  W  A  A  J  R  R  T  U  V  D
W  S  D  B  A  Y  I  X  O  N  I  N  O  O  F  B  N
X  U  U  J  L  S  N  W  N  G  O  R  E  Y  P  L  E
I  E  C  S  W  T  V  V  G  W  A  I  C  F  V  N  N
V  Z  A  E  A  O  L  A  L  W  P  J  D  B  F  I  T
J  A  F  L  Y  N  N  E  K  R  E  T  T  E  L  X  K
N  V  G  K  C  E  L  A  G  D  J  X  V  M  V  M  B
X  C  B  F  A  S  X  R  C  L  E  I  X  L  I  P  A
```

NAAS	COBH	BIRR
GOREY	ATHLONE	WEXFORD
CLONMEL	LEIXLIP	WICKLOW
MALAHIDE	BUNCRANA	MULLINGAR
CELBRIDGE	DUNGARVAN	PORTLAOISE
BALBRIGGAN	GREYSTONES	LETTERKENNY
CLAREGALWAY	DUNSHAUGHLIN	

■■ LANDMARKS

```
B F R A C N E L G Z J G B C B S U W M
E A T I O W J L W I L D A D I I R X O
Q R D S N Y D C E G A B Y P H B W G U
M A J G A G Q U P H Y N Y I H V R K R
B M Y W L F O T N A S K T B E K E E N
L E S G Q O L F W A K A H S R Q H R E
A N C U G D U E K F E Z C N R T O K O
R N Z V A H S G B E R N R F G I M L Q
N O R G A U D N H C R D G M O P N H T
E C R Y A E N A H O I R A U B K R G S
Y Y L C E H A R X P E N Y B S N C U P
Q C A D H I L G X X S M A X S D U O E
L L D Y W H S W P R M D Y T Z J W L R
D F V J N I I E R D I Z P E I U T A R
F A E Q N V N N X T L R O X G T K D I
F B E L T S A C N I L B U D W C G N N
D K F H V R R V L G S U L Q S B W E S
B P Z U R D A K N E B L U B N E B L E
C G F Q Q A A Q P G T S K E L L I G G
```

MOHER	LOUGH	MOURNE
BLARNEY	SKELLIG	GLENCAR
CAUSEWAY	SPERRINS	NEWGRANGE
CONNEMARA	BENBULBEN	DUN AENGUS
GLENDALOUGH	GIANTS RING	ARAN ISLANDS
DUBLIN CASTLE	RING OF KERRY	ROCK OF CASHEL
SKERRIES MILLS	TITANIC BELFAST	

NORTHERN IRELAND

```
H G A M O Q A N E M Y L L A B C A F
N J H E Y L X H G D O O W Y L O H Q
X D Z M U A G S F E G D I R B N A B
D N O M C A R R I C K F E R G U S X
B D Z O M M Y E V W L T Y E Y F U F
A U O R N P R A N Z J S X D D N C D
L R A W F N W O T S L A D N A R U U
L F O P N M E X X F T F N O V D A I
Y U I G O P N E N R A L C D A O Y J
M A G H E R A F E L T E C N M W J S
O G H S Y S T T Z F K B I O I Q N M
N M R T V T V A R F S N F L L I Q P
E T V H M C J L D I G G F T I L Y S
Y N E N I A R E L O C U U W I Z I I
A I K F R J B P W L W K I V O S F U
G M V T T L I S B U R N W I L J R J
S Z Z E N A G R U L Y Z W E L M N W
N O O V A V B N S E S J J A V N T V
```

NEWRY
ARMAGH
BELFAST
HOLYWOOD
PORTADOWN
LONDONDERRY
RANDALSTOWN

OMAGH
ANTRIM
LISBURN
COLERAINE
BANBRIDGE
MAGHERAFELT
CARRICKFERGUS

LARNE
LURGAN
LIMAVADY
BALLYMENA
BALLYMONEY
DOWNPATRICK

SYMBOLS

```
N F R B S V O K C L A J M U S E V R W
N V M A T W L V I W K O H E B B F E C
H C B I P L E H T T A M G C H M I E F
G P U E A P P C L G B Y B K I R L W S
U K J K T G R O E K R A R P E D J Y G
I X I C R H A A C L Z G W T D A S J V
N U S I I R C D H D T N L I Y N C Y C
N Y C C C H C C L Q I F P Z T L C F
E T Y A K R A F P C A C C R L W O X R
S R L K J T U E L F O N I C O K V E C
S S N D S U N L E H Q A A L R C E X G
V H G A L E L L I H S D F U C O R S K
T O N K Y T I N I R T H N B A R S D L
S A L R V M D M E G O S Z Y I M N S F
H G A D D A L C R U U I Q E O A C L R
T O R A I B G E N M J R W G L H K E W
G A E I L G E D C P J I N E Q S G S E
E C A H Z N L U X O P D R A H F X R P
C I L E A G B X E U U I I Z U K A F U
```

HARP	EIRE	GREEN
CELTIC	GAELIC	CLOVER
FIDDLE	IRELAND	GAEILGE
SHAMROCK	CLADDAGH	GUINNESS
LEPRACHAUN	ST PATRICK	WOLF HOUND
SHILLELAGH	TRINITY KNOT	CELTIC CROSS
IRISH DANCING	CEAD MILE FAILTE	

Conclusion

Phew!

What a journey, I bet we could all do with some soda bread and a warm stew!

I hope that this book has given some insight into the wonders of Ireland and also left you eager to learn more!

Let's recap with 10 of my favorite facts, shall we? Why not make a note of your favorites too?

1. The mythical explanation for the amazing Giants Causeway is that an Irish Giant created it to challenge a Scottish giant to a battle, and what's left today, is all that was left after their confrontation!

2. Dublin was founded by Vikings back in 841 and is home to the biggest Viking cemetery outside of Scandinavia (okay, that's technically two facts!).

3. Wearing green on St. Patrick's Day will make you invisible to cheeky leprechauns, and if you wear any other color, they will pinch you!

4. The Celtic Harp is on Ireland's Euro coins!

5. Some believe that hurling was invented to train warriors in the Middle Ages, which may well be true, because the Marine Corps have two teams of their own, and they're modern-day warriors!

6. Gaelic is one of Europe's oldest languages!

7. Irishman Hans Sloane invented chocolate milk back in the 17th century after he was inspired by the chocolate water that was being enjoyed in Jamaica. But he first sold his tasty recipe as a medication!

8. Aran sweaters were created on the Aran islands just off the west coast of Ireland and were knit by hand using the wool from the island's sheep! It was often the wives of fishermen who made them in order to help keep their husbands nice and toasty while out on their boats!

9. In Ireland, some bachelor's degrees based on job-oriented subjects are free to Irish, United Kingdom (UK), European Union (EU), and Swiss students! International students applying for a course that isn't free can apply for bursaries and scholarships!

10. *The Lord of the Rings* was said to be heavily influenced by some of Ireland's beautiful landscapes. The franchise's roots in Ireland run so deep that festivals held in the Burren are believed to have inspired J. R. R. Tolkien to write the books!

Why not make a note of some of your favorite facts, too, so you can share them with friends?

Favorite fact	Chapter number

Right! That's about it from me; I'll just leave you with a little game below to test your knowledge and memory!

Two Facts and a Lie

Feel free to check back through the associated chapter before you test your memory by circling the lie that's hidden among the two facts!

Chapter 3

1. The type of rock that the columns at Giant's Causeway are made from is called "Tholeiitic basalt," and it's also found on the moon!

2. Parts of the Causeway can also be found in England!

3. The Causeway was first discovered in the 17th century by the Bishop of Derry!

Chapter 7

1. Once finished, the Titanic was a whopping 882 feet and 6 inches long and weighed 46,000 tons!

2. Cobh, in County Cork, was the final pick-up for the Titanic's passengers, and the ship was so big that passengers from Cobh had to board using smaller ships that took them aboard!

3. 123 first-class passengers boarded the Titanic from Cobh!

Chapter 12

1. Dublin native Bram Stoker invented the werewolf!

2. Oscar Wilde was born in Dublin!

3. C. S. Lewis was born in Belfast!

Ready for the answers?

Last warning!

The lies are

1. Parts of the Giant Causeway can actually be found in Scotland, not England!

2. 123 passengers *did* board the Titanic from Cobh, but only three of them were first class!

3. Dublin native Bram Stoker invented Dracula, not the werewolf!

I hope you've had fun kids, and you're excited to continue learning about Ireland. Take care of yourselves, and we'll see you for the next fact book!

Henry.

Bonus: Coloring Mandalas

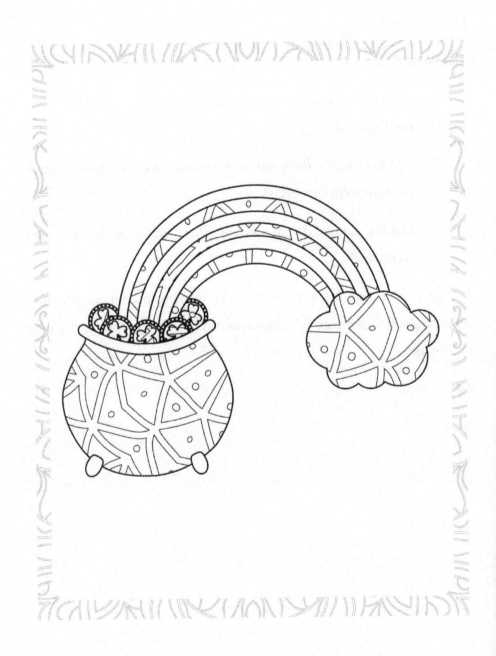

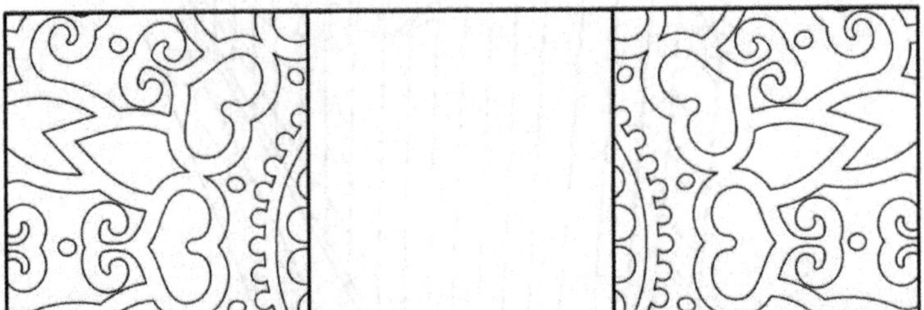

References

About Titanic Belfast. (n.d.). Titanic Belfast.
https://www.titanicbelfast.com/explore/about-titanic-belfast/

Artefacts. (n.d.). Titanic Belfast. https://www.titanicbelfast.com/history-of-titanic/artefacts/

Augello, C. (2023, July 25). *9 traditional Irish crafts & their fascinating history*. ConnollyCove. https://www.connollycove.com/traditional-irish-crafts-history/

Badnjarevic, D. (2020, August 7). *The highest mountains in Ireland: 11 mighty peaks to conquer in your lifetime*. The Irish Road Trip.
https://www.theirishroadtrip.com/highest-mountains-in-ireland/

Belfast Agreement facts for kids. (n.d.). Kiddle.
https://kids.kiddle.co/Belfast_Agreement

Carter, S. (2024). *14 top geography facts about Ireland to share with students*. Twinkl. https://www.twinkl.co.uk/blog/14-top-geography-facts-about-ireland-to-share-with-students

Ceili Feiles and Fleadh traditional Irish festivals. (n.d.). Discovering Ireland. https://www.discoveringireland.com/ceili-feiles-and-fleadh-traditional-irish-festivals/#:~:text=Two%20of%20the%20oldest%20traditional

The Cliffs of Moher: 15 must-know facts about an incredible Irish landmark. (n.d.). Irish Expressions. https://www.irish-expressions.com/cliffs-of-moher.html

Cobh: Titanic's last port of call. (2022). Ireland.com.
https://www.ireland.com/en-gb/magazine/built-heritage/titanic-in-cobh/#:~:text=For%20the%20123%20people%20that

Derry. (2023). *Ireland's castles & their fascinating facts*. Vagabond Tours of Ireland. https://vagabondtoursofireland.com/blog/ireland-castles-fascinating-facts

Dunseverick Castle. (n.d.). National Trust. https://www.nationaltrust.org.uk/visit/northern-ireland/castles-forts/dunseverick-castle

8 facts about study in Ireland. (2022). Edwise International. https://www.edwiseinternational.com/study-abroad-resources/8-facts-about-study-in-ireland.aspx

8 fun facts about the Irish language. (2015, March 11). Mental Floss. https://www.mentalfloss.com/article/49480/8-fun-facts-about-irish-language#:~:text=By%20Arika%20Okrent%20%7C%20Mar%2017%2C%20%202023%2C%2010%3A00

11 fun facts about hurling. (2015, March 14). Play Hurling. https://playhurling.com/11-fun-facts-about-hurling/

Fact sheet on the conflict in and about Northern Ireland. (2007). https://cain.ulster.ac.uk/victims/docs/group/htr/day_of_reflection/htr_060 7c.pdf

Fantastic lighthouse facts. (n.d.). Great Lighthouses of Ireland. https://www.greatlighthouses.com/stories/fantastic-lighthouse-facts/#:~:text=Wexford%27s%20Hook%20Head%20Lighthouse%20was

5 fun things to see at the Titanic Museum Belfast. (2020). Attractiontickets.com. https://www.attractiontickets.com/en/latest-news/5-fun-things-see-titanic-museum-belfast

5 traditional crafts of Ireland. (2020, September 10). Shutterspeed Ireland. https://www.shutterspeedireland.com/crafts-of-ireland/

Flora and fauna. (2013, August 23). Burren and Cliffs of Moher Geopark. https://www.burrengeopark.ie/learn-engage/geology-of-the-burren/flora-and-fauna/

Fun facts about Blarney Castle. (2011, December 28). Tenon Tours. https://www.tenontours.com/blog/fun-facts-about-blarney-castle/

The geology of the Burren. (2013, August 22). The Burren and Cliffs of Moher UNESCO Global Geopark. https://www.burrengeopark.ie/learn-engage/the-geology-of-the-burren/

The Giants Causeway in 10 amazing facts. (2021, February 15). Walking Hiking Blog. https://www.hillwalktours.com/walking-hiking-blog/the-giants-causeway-in-10-amazing-facts/

Griffin, S. (2021, December 27). *35 fun St Patricks Day facts for kids.* Little Learning Corner. https://littlelearningcorner.com/2021/12/35-fun-st-patricks-day-facts-for-kids.html

Harlitz-Kern, E. (2015, November 5). *10 things you should know about the Book of Kells.* Book Riot. https://bookriot.com/10-things-know-book-kells/

Hesse, R. (2023, January 16). *Ireland's Great Hunger: 13 facts about the 19th-century potato famine that devastated the Emerald Isle.* Mental Floss. https://www.mentalfloss.com/posts/irish-potato-famine-facts

Hofer, A. (2023, August 20). *Top 10 mad facts about Gaelic football you never knew.* Meanwhile in Ireland. https://meanwhileinireland.com/top-10-mad-facts-about-gaelic-football-you-never-knew/

Hook Lighthouse: 5 things you didn't know. (n.d.). Great Lighthouses of Ireland. https://www.greatlighthouses.com/stories/hook-lighthouse-5-things-you-didnt-know/#:~:text=Hook%20Lighthouse%20was%20purpose%2Dbuilt

The importance of the small stream network in Ireland. (2019, July 16). Catchments. https://www.catchments.ie/the-importance-of-the-small-stream-network-in-ireland/

Ireland facts: All about the Emerald Isle. (n.d.). National Geographic Kids. https://www.natgeokids.com/uk/discover/geography/countries/facts-about-ireland/#:~:text=Ireland%20is%20known%20for%20its

Ireland's lighthouses. (2020). Ireland.com. https://www.ireland.com/en-us/magazine/built-heritage/lighthouses-in-ireland/

Ireland's most recognizable sites in pop culture and films. (n.d.). Global Experiences. https://www.globalexperiences.com/blog/ireland-pop-culture-sites

Irish fairies: Irish folklore, myth & legend. (2023, July 7). ShanOre Irish Jewelry. https://www.shanore.com/blog/irish-fairies/

Irish holidays you should know about. (2022). Irish American Mom. https://www.irishamericanmom.com/irish-holidays-you-should-know-about/

Irish language facts for kids. (n.d.). Kiddle. https://kids.kiddle.co/Irish_language#:~:text=Irish%20language%20facts %20for%20kids%201%20Figures%20There

Irish scientists and inventors. (n.d.). IPOI. https://www.ipoi.gov.ie/en/understanding-ip/student-zone/irish-scientists-inventors/#:~:text=Walton%20and%20Cockcroft%20had%20vindicated

Janet. (2016, June 17). *5 fascinating facts about the Cliffs of Moher.* Wild Rover Tours. https://wildrovertours.com/blog/5-fascinating-facts-cliffs-moher/

Kennedy, L. (2023). *Titanic by the numbers: From construction to disaster to discovery.* HISTORY. https://www.history.com/news/titanic-facts-construction-passengers-sinking-discovery

kevmrc. (2023). *17 must-read Ireland education facts [100% true].* Kevmrc.com. https://www.kevmrc.com/ireland-education-facts

Kilkenny Castle: 10 amazing facts about an ancient Irish structure. (n.d.). Irish Expressions. https://www.irish-expressions.com/kilkenny-castle.html

Kirby, T. (2016, February 9). *32 little truths about the Burren.* Heart of Burren Walks. https://www.heartofburrenwalks.com/burren-facts

Leprechauns. (n.d.). Discovering Ireland. https://www.discoveringireland.com/leprechauns/#:~:text=In%20Irish%2 0folklore%20a%20Leprechaun

Licata, J. (2024). *19 unbelievable facts about Fota Wildlife Park.* Facts. https://facts.net/world/landmarks/19-unbelievable-facts-about-fota-wildlife-park/

Manning, E. (2021, February 23). *14 of the best Irish movies for your next family movie night.* MyKidsTime. https://www.mykidstime.com/entertainment/best-irish-movies-for-families/

The most famous person from every county of Ireland. (2023). Ireland before You Die. https://www.irelandbeforeyoudie.com/32-famous-irish-people-the-most-famous-person-from-every-county/

9 interesting Dublin Zoo facts. (n.d.). Twinkl. https://www.twinkl.co.uk/blog/interesting-dublin-zoo-facts

9 wee facts about the Irish Sea. (2021). WoodChart. https://www.woodchart.com/blogs/news/9-wee-facts-about-the-irish-sea

Northern Ireland celebrates ten years of a Titanic impact. (2022). Titanic Belfast. https://www.titanicbelfast.com/news/northern-ireland-celebrates-ten-years-of-a-titanic-impact/

Ó Murchadh, O. (2023). *21 of the most unusual, weird and interesting facts about Dublin.* The Irish Road Trip. https://www.theirishroadtrip.com/facts-about-dublin/

O'Connor, R. (2021). *8 of Ireland's best outdoor wildlife parks, zoos and sanctuaries to help plan your next trip.* The Irish Post. https://www.irishpost.com/travel/8-of-irelands-best-outdoor-wildlife-parks-zoos-and-sanctuaries-to-help-plan-your-next-trip-209576

O'Hara, A. K. (2023a, July 6). *41 most famous Irish people of all time.* The Irish Road Trip. https://www.theirishroadtrip.com/famous-irish-people/

O'Hara, K. (2023b, July 10). *32 of the most famous landmarks in Ireland.* The Irish Road Trip. https://www.theirishroadtrip.com/famous-landmarks-in-ireland/

O'Hara, K. (2024). *Irish mythology: 12 myths and legends I was told growing up in Ireland.* The Irish Road Trip. https://www.theirishroadtrip.com/irish-mythology/

Pauline. (2023). *27+ incredible facts about Dublin that will blow your mind.* BeeLoved City. https://www.beelovedcity.com/facts-dublin

Rainbolt, D. (2021, April 8). *Ireland's marine & coastal wildlife.* Wilderness Ireland. https://www.wildernessireland.com/blog/irelands-marine-coastal-wildlife/

Roller, S. (2022). *10 facts about the Book of Kells*. History Hit. https://www.historyhit.com/culture/facts-about-the-book-of-kells/

Sarah. (2023, July 12). *Top 10 ancient sites in Ireland*. Insight Guides. https://www.insightguides.com/inspire-me/blog/top-10-ancient-sites-in-ireland#:~:text=Of%20all%20the%20ancient%20sites

7 facts about Irish Dance. (n.d.). Asheville Performing Arts Academy. https://theapaa.com/blog/7-facts-about-irish-dance

17 fascinating facts about Irish music. (2013, March 6). Soundscaping Source. https://soundscapingsource.com/17-fascinating-facts-about-irish-music/

17 weird and wonderful Irish inventions. (2017, September 1). Claddagh Design. https://www.claddaghdesign.com/en-gb/blogs/irish-interest/17-weird-and-wonderful-irish-inventions

17th century city walls. (n.d.). Discover Northern Ireland. https://discovernorthernireland.com/things-to-do/17th-century-city-walls-p685431

10 amazing animal species native to Ireland. (2024). Ireland before You Die. https://www.irelandbeforeyoudie.com/10-amazing-animal-species-native-to-ireland/

Ten fantastic facts about the Wild Atlantic Way. (n.d.). Discover Ireland. https://www.discoverireland.ie/wild-atlantic-way/fantastic-facts-about-the-wild-atlantic-way

10 Irish inventions that changed the world. (2015, November 9). Think Business. https://www.thinkbusiness.ie/articles/10-world-changing-irish-inventions/

10 surprising facts about the Giant's Causeway you probably didn't know! (2023, September 11). Cowfield Design. https://cowfielddesign.com/blogs/cowfield-design/10-surprising-facts-about-the-giants-causeway-you-probably-didnt-know

13 exceptional Irish scientists you absolutely need to know. (2015, November 13). Silicon Republic.

https://www.siliconrepublic.com/innovation/irish-scientists-discoveries-science-week

Titanic's Irish roots. (2019, June 24). Crystal Travel and Tours. https://www.crystal-travel.com/blog/titanicsirishroots/

Top 10 facts about Saint Patrick's Day! (n.d.). Fun Kids. https://www.funkidslive.com/learn/top-10-facts/top-10-facts-about-saint-patricks-day/

The troubles facts for kids. (n.d.). Kiddle. https://kids.kiddle.co/The_Troubles

12 Celtic symbols and meanings explained. (2023). Shanore. https://www.shanore.com/blog/12-celtic-symbols-and-meanings-explained/

20 surprising facts about Irish food you probably didn't know. (2023, May 16). Irish Food Hub. https://irishfoodhub.com/20-surprising-facts-about-irish-food-you-probably-didnt-know/

Vaal, D. D. (2023, April 20). *Ireland's first astronaut can't wait to fly Irish flag in space.* Irish Star. https://www.irishstar.com/news/ireland-news/irelands-first-astronaut-cant-wait-29757260

What are the rivers of Ireland? (n.d.). Twinkl. https://www.twinkl.co.uk/teaching-wiki/rivers-of-ireland#:~:text=The%20largest%20river%20in%20Ireland

Where in Ireland is Vikings filmed. (2021, February 1). Emerald Heritage. https://emerald-heritage.com/blog/2017/where-in-ireland-is-vikings-filmed

Whitnear, A. (n.d.). *10 exciting Dublin facts.* Twinkl. https://www.twinkl.ch/blog/10-exciting-dublin-facts

Wickham, C. (2020a, March 18). *Top 10 Irish writers of all time.* Ireland before You Die. https://www.irelandbeforeyoudie.com/top-10-irish-writers-of-all-time/

Wickham, C. (2020b, October 20). *Top 10 facts about the Irish language you never knew.* Ireland before You Die.

https://www.irelandbeforeyoudie.com/top-10-facts-about-the-irish-language-you-never-knew/

Wild Atlantic WayLighthouse kids. (n.d.). Kiddle.
https://kids.kiddle.co/Wild_Atlantic_Way